GW00986033

Mastering
The Inner Game of Golf

'INTO THE ZONE'

Interactive Mind Coaching
Golf Psychology Course

with
Robert Bourne
Sports Psychologist

Naturally You
Publishing

United Kingdom

Mastering The Inner Game of Golf

Copyright © 2009 by Robert Bourne

All rights reserved. No part of this book may be reproduced or transmitted in any form or by any means without written permission of the author.

The accompanying 5 CD set containing part 2 and 3 of the mind coaching system is available from: **www.into-thezone.co.uk**

PGA golf professionals can train as an 'INTO THE ZONE' Golf Psychology Trainer - details at: **www.into-thezone.co.uk**

Published and Distributed by
Naturally You Publishing

ISBN 978-0-9561159-8-0

A catalogue of this publication is available from the British Library

Naturally You
Publishing

Table of Contents

About this Multimedia Course

Mastering the Inner Game of Golf contains a book and five interactive mind coaching CDs for the golfer. This interactive course will take you 'Into the Zone' revolutionising the mental approach for today's golfer, enabling you to achieve your full golfing potential.

"I take people 'Into the Zone' so that they can achieve excellence within their game of golf. When you play you need to learn how to 'Get out of the Way!" Robert Bourne

This multimedia mind coaching course outlines:

- How to master the thoughts in your mind that prevent you from achieving your best
- Creating a whole body and mind that is working in unity as one whole person; creating a relaxed focused golf swing
- How to use visualisation in relation to picturing the golf shot that you want to achieve
- How to get into 'The Zone' before you take your shot
- How to enjoy your golf game no matter how you are playing! You will learn how to maintain enjoyment on the course using 'one shot at a time'

- How to become a relaxed golfer – mind, emotions and body
- How to be generous to others and be kind to yourself

I see sports as an expression of creativity. To fully experience the joy contained within this aspect of life you will need to go deep within yourself. Whenever you are enjoying your performance, your game, your sport you have enjoyed the inner union, you have become whole within yourself. That is what all great successful sports people have discovered. This wholeness only comes about through connecting and releasing life's full inner power which is contained within you right now.

I have personally discovered this inner goldmine, this place of unlimited potential and it is this which I am going to share with you. I decided to find a way to share this special experience with as many people as possible. This is the reason why I have created 'Into the Zone' as an interactive experience. One thing I have learnt is that whatever you learn in this world becomes a gift for mankind. It is only when you share this gift with others that you can feel the joy, the happiness that is released when another person has that 'Aha' moment, that moment of realisation which brings them to a place of sharing that knowledge, that skill, that inner self realisation. I think this is a sign of a great teacher. I thank you for allowing me to share with you 'The Inner Secret'.

It is when the teaching, the skill becomes self-realised on the inside is it only truly learnt. It then becomes alive inside of you, it becomes an inner resource which you can depend upon, which will manifest in your life when you need it automatically without the struggle the conscious mind so often brings to the present moment.

I am now joyfully alive because I have this opportunity to share with you this age old secret, this gift I have discovered. To fully join me in this wonderful experience of mastering the inner game you will need to trust me and work through the interactive CD set which will take you deeply into all aspects of your game of golf in the coaching format I am presenting. So just for now, suspend your judgement - you have nothing to lose and everything to gain. If you do this a transformation will occur within you that will pleasantly surprise you.

This Interactive Course is divided into Three Parts

Step1: Theoretical understanding through reading and studying this book – the knowledge.

Step 2: Using the first CD which will teach you how to get 'Into the Zone'. Once you have discovered this inner experience you will learn how to master your mind and emotions. This is extremely important for you when creating excellence in your game of golf. This first CD needs to be used every day for twenty-one days. Please trust me when I say that this stage is the crucial key to unlocking the knowledge contained within the book. If you bypass this stage you are likely to fail. I hope I have stressed the importance of the repetition required to achieve this new skill.

Step 3: What to do when you are in the zone. It is one thing achieving the state of being 'In the Zone'; it is another to know what to do when you get there. The remaining four CDs cover the four different aspects of your game which are on CD2 'The Long Game', on CD3 'The Short Game' on CD4 'Discovering Perfect Putting' and CD5 'How to Excel in Tournaments and Competitions'.

These final four CDs teach you how to become creative and cover the key areas of your game of golf. This is where this interactive course is different from most other golf training courses I have looked at. Most other courses stop at stage one because they just provide you knowledge contained within a book. They don't provide you the key of how to change your consciousness, how to access your unconscious mind and how to draw on the creative force that is contained deep within your life. So regard this course as a lock and key. The book is the lock; the CD set is the key to unlocking the secret of achieving excellence.

The way to approach learning this course is to first read the book several times and at the same time as reading the book, for a period of twenty-one days use your practice CD1 'Getting your Mind to Work for You'. You will be practicing and experiencing entering 'Into the Zone'.

You will be loading your conscious mind with knowledge and information through reading the book. The information in the book will teach you how your mind works in relation to your emotions and physical body. It is very important to load your conscious mind with the information contained within the book for you will be taking this information into your subconscious mind and installing a new software program within you that will enable you to produce your very best on the golf course under any circumstances, in any situation.

So for twenty-one days read the book and use the CD1 every day.

After twenty-one days go on to using the final four CDs. Just follow the instructions that are on the introduction of each CD.

Caution

This course comes with the following warning:

"Beware - as a result of using this course you could reduce your score dramatically whilst becoming a happy and relaxed golfer".

The accompanying 5 CD set

If have only bought the book then to be able to get the result in your golf game, as described in step 2 and step 3 of this unique mind coaching system, please order the 5 CD set. Thank you.

Order your 5 CD mind coaching set from
www.into-thezone .co.uk

Neuroscience in Sports Performance

The scientific findings that are at the cutting edge for achieving excellence in sports performance provide us with the evidence that links what psychologists have been reporting for many years. This exciting breakthrough has created a bridge in the understanding of mind training, which now incorporates the conscious and unconscious mind. Both parts of the mind need to be understood to achieve mastery over your chosen sport. In the 2008 Olympic Games in Beijing, China, Japan used this new method of mind training to accomplish optimum sports performance.

Some athletes excel on big occasions while others do not. What's behind the difference? Efforts to find out are being made in the world of neuroscience. Japanese swimmers did well in the Beijing Olympics. Behind their success was little publicised guidance from a neuroscientist and this is what we are going to look at as our starting point in mastering the inner game of golf; the scientific evidence.

In the realm of the mind and emotions we enter a realm that is quite intangible inasmuch as it is not physical, although we all know it's real. We all know we have thoughts, we all know we have emotions. The other common truth of our existence is that we have all had an education; however that education did not teach us about the fundamental truths of the human being, which are the workings of the mind and the emotions. Today's age is heavily dependent upon scientific evidence so before I take you into the inner realm known as 'Into the Zone' this intangible space that can enable you to achieve more than just your mind and emotions alone, we need to have an entry point of acceptance. This is why I would like to start with what science now understands. The world of neuroscience is now very close to hitting this ultimate truth; the invisible realm of the higher intelligence that exists 'within the zone' within you.

When in the past I have shared the findings of neuroscience, which are scientific proofs of how our mind and emotions affect our performance, many people have found it difficult to believe. What I ask you to do first of all to enable this interactive course to provide a tremendous transformation within you, is that I ask you to open your mind to the realm of possibility. For this moment and during this course just accept totally the scientific evidence which I am now about to share. This will become your starting point of your new transformation, of your new journey in discovering excellence and peak performance within your game of golf. The amazing thing that will happen is that once your have learnt this new skill that you will have to practice, as it is a skill to be learnt, your game of golf will improve automatically - so will many other areas of your life! Just as when you were learning a new shot, learning how to chip the ball for the very first time, you had to practice. This same principle also applies to training your mind and emotions.

When it comes to anything that you wish to experience auto-matically, like a swing, like a new way of thinking, a new emotional reaction, to enable that to become an automatic response within your life you will first have to erase what already exists, that which you do not want, that which is not serving you well. So the first scientific fact I would like to share with you is that it takes twenty-one times of repeated behaviour or twenty-one days of repeated behaviour for the brain to form a new neural pathway that will repeat the new swing, the new way of thinking, the new emotional pattern automatically without you making any effort. This is the first scientific truth and it will help you in your practice to take this understanding to whatever you are learning. Once the neural pathway has formed in the brain, with constant practice it becomes deeply ingrained. With this realisation you can now have an understanding why old negative patterns that you no longer want are so difficult to erase. In fact once a learnt pattern becomes an unconscious memory the harder you try consciously to overcome it the more resistance there is unconsciously to it being removed. There is a 'Law of Reverse Effect' which states when the will and the inner mind are in conflict the inner mind always wins. This means that when a person thinks he cannot do something and then tries, the more he tries to do it the less it is possible to achieve. In the conflict between the will and the inner mind the force of the inner mind produces about four times more energy than the will, so by willpower alone it's virtually impossible to change ingrained patterns of action, thought and emotional reactions.

The key to you changing is to learn a new way of dealing with your unconscious mind and the very first thing you will need to do is to learn how to get access to the realm of your unconscious mind. You will do this through learning how to achieve the alpha state of mind, which you will experience through continuous practice using the first CD1 in this course, 'Getting Your Mind to Work For You' learning the experience of entering the zone.

So now let us look at what these new scientific discoveries are and how they have been applied to professional athletes to enable them to achieve a greater performance than they could have previously achieved, before using these findings to train their brain.

In Canada they have what is known as 'Brain Training Gyms'. Olympic athletes are saying after experiencing the methods that every athlete should learn how to train their brain. These brain training gyms are also being used for business people. The methods used in these gyms are contained in this course, although in a different format.

What is the secret to performing well under pressure? It is revealed in the front line of brain training research and it is this that we are now going to look at.

Brain training gyms are something that is of particular interest to me personally and I am looking into the possibility of introducing this idea into the UK in the near future. Just imagine it. You go for a training session with your golf pro, he teaches you about weight transference so that you can get greater distance on your shot. The second half of the lesson you enter the brain training gym; you put on the headset and carry out certain bio feedback exercises to train you to achieve the alpha state of mind.

On important occasions such as job interviews or exams, teeing off from the first tee or an important putt on the putting green, people tend to get nervous and fail to perform at their full ability. In the world of sports even a moment of hesitation or worry crossing the mind can seriously affect one's performance. Athletes train so that they can perform at their best in competitions under any conditions. An incorrect belief which is commonly held today is that willpower and determination are the keys to overcoming anxiety. Today sports training is incorporating the latest findings in neuroscience. The idea is to train athlete's brains so that they can control their physical performance with their minds. This is what is happening in neuroscience today and you will learn how to do this on this course. Once you have discovered that truth, that ability, you will then have the faith and the belief to take the next step which is discovering the power that exists when you go 'Into the Zone'. All of these techniques and methods you are going to learn on this course. But we are going to take this one step at a time.

In the latest training athletes now work not only on enhancing their physical performance and skills but also on controlling their minds under stress. For example, what brain activity causes the body to tighten up and what kind of mind set is needed to perform at one's best when it counts. As scientists gradually learn more about the mechanism linking the brain and the body, athletes try to use such findings to improve their performance.

A conference entitled 'Symposium on Sports and the Brain' at Waseda University in Japan in March 2009 was attended by many top sports professionals around the world to discover the latest findings in neuroscience. They discussed how the brain and body can be put into top condition for competitions and what stimuli should be applied to the brain and muscles to get 'out of the slump'. All sports people are very fortunate because the head of this new research project Eiichi Naito says they are applying their findings to sports people first in preference to business application. He said this is the most interesting discovery in brain science studies that he has ever experienced. As you are a sports person you are benefiting from the latest proven discoveries in neuroscience.

This book is revolutionary because it was only earlier this year that I was informed of these studies by my friend in Japan. Simply put this means the training techniques on this course are the same as used by 2008 Olympic gold medallists!

Shawn Youngstedt, a professor from the University of South Carolina was most excited about the Japanese discoveries about what might be happening in the brain in terms of influencing the skills in sports performance.

Neuroscience produced amazing results in the Beijing Olympics. Japan's national swimming team won 5 Olympic medals. Behind this success was a little known experiment. At the Japanese Institute of Sports Science in Tokyo four months before the Olympics, Japan's head coach was worried about many swimmers losing speed just before the finish and struggling to improve their times. At an Olympic qualifying meet in April 2008 one of the Japanese breast stroke swimmers was ahead of the world record pace but slowed down in the last 50 metres. The Japanese swimming team head coach Norimasa Hirai noticed that three of the swimmers he trains seemed to lose speed once they thought the goal was near. He and the other swimming coaches suspected that the problem was something other than physical strength or skill. In the hope that brain science could help he sought advice from an eminent neurosurgeon Dr Niriyuki Hayashi. He was invited to give a lecture to the team two months before the Olympic Games. More than 40 swimmers and coaches came to listen. Hayashi said that he had come to talk about the strategy of winning a medal at the forthcoming Olympics from the viewpoint of neuroscience. He explained how brain activity affects physical activity. He stressed that thinking a goal is near can trigger a loss of speed. When playing golf or in any sport the same principles apply. Hayashi said that in a 400 metre race the swimmer might start thinking about the goal after 300 metres. He says the world 'goal' has a negative effect on the brain and causes the top athletic ability displayed until then to disappear.

This particular truth is specifically related to the concept of winning, of achieving. The golfer by nature is familiar with 18 holes and is constantly checking and measuring his own performance in relation to par and to the other players. He has an idea of what he needs to achieve to be successful in this round of golf. Coming up to the 18th hole, maybe at the 16th he has a pretty good idea of how he is doing, his mind constantly checking and measuring, attaching itself to the final objective, the winning or losing of this round of golf. You are going to learn the negative effects of checking and measuring what you are doing and being attached to the outcome of winning and how this is causing you not to perform at your best potential.

Logically it doesn't make sense - we all would like to win, we may even have a great passion to achieve phenomenal results. Who wouldn't like to win a medal? Who wouldn't like fellow golfers to say he or she is a superb player? Winning attracts always being invited to be part of the team. So logically it makes sense to have a desire to win, but as you will soon discover your objective is going to be to learn how to be in the present moment like all top PGA pros have discovered, being in the now, just one shot at a time is the real secret to obtaining excellence in the game of golf.

So let's look at this from a neuro-scientific point of view. For an athlete to perform at their best, at their top physical ability, yes, they must first have the desire to do so. This desire comes from the psycho-motor centre, the frontal lobe of the brain which sends this information to their spatial perception centre. This activates nerves in the brain that are associated with reward. This enhances concentration and creates a circuit linking the reward related nerves and the motor nerve. Your mind is now telling your body what to do subconsciously. However when those nerves receive information that the goal is near the mind judges that the task has been achieved and in effect the brain believes the goal has been accomplished. When this happens the original desire to perform at one's best gets switched off within the brain. This in turn switches off the motor nerve because they judge that the task has been achieved. This breaks the circuit and the body can no longer perform at its best.

The secret you are going to learn to do is to stay in the present moment where you are always sending the message from your desire centre to your brain for it to perform at its optimal best. This will maintain the link within the brain to send this information through your nervous system into the muscles to enable the body to carry out the required response in your swing, to produce the outcome you have just pictured.

To give an example of how this works in daily life, I was giving dictation to my secretary for this first chapter of the book. Coming near to the end my secretary relaxed her mind and lost concentration and started making errors, so I had to kid her that there was a lot more to do yet and that we were nowhere near completing this section. She instantly went back to optimal performance, to her normal standard of excellence and of course the task was completed a couple of paragraphs later. We both burst into laughter when I shared with her "Do you understand now what I am talking about?" She had to agree. There is no substitute for personal experience!

There's a lot of information here so let's review at this moment what actually is happening. In simple terms you have a desire which is made up of thoughts and mental images. Your will provides this information, which is contained within the frontal lobe of the brain. That information then gets transferred to the unconscious mind, which then selects the appropriate swing memory automatically to produce that which you want; the shot outcome you wish to achieve. Your subconscious mind will mirror the original thoughts you had before you took your shot. The swing then occurs automatically becoming an automatic mind body reaction. This is why you need to examine your thoughts very carefully.

Your thoughts get transformed through neuro messengers, various hormones, and electrical energy information is carried through the nervous system into the muscles and the swing is the result. The very best performance or outcome, of hitting the ball towards the target, with your mind out of the way, will create the result of achieving the very best shot you can accomplish at this time. The outcome starts in the mind, the pictured shot focused upon the target.

This is going to be your new goal, to be able to repeat this from shot to shot with the attitude that each shot is your first shot. Your new mental attitude is going to be to learn how to have the ability to let go of the outcome, to enter the realm of acceptance, this is what is known as staying in the present moment.

Why is staying in 'the now' so important? If you are concerned about thinking about the outcome of your last shot you are loading your conscious mind with that information; you are in fact asking your mind to recreate that bad shot again.

This is how it works. That negative information will then be transferred to the inner mind which in turn sends information to the physical body. You keep thinking about it, you keep dwelling on it, you keep programming yourself to perform that very same bad shot once again.

I hope you are beginning to see what I am trying to share. You then try and make your current shot and your mind now has two sets of information; to repeat the last bad shot and to play the shot you are about to hit. It is a bit like loading a gun, not firing it and trying to put another shell into it before you have pulled the trigger.

Because the mind takes the information literally, as the inner unconscious mind only exists 'in the now' which is another new understanding, a new truth that you have to embrace, it is your inner mind that produces the shot you experience; this is the source of your true power. The inner mind orchestrates an infinity of events, the lie of the ball, the fairway or putting green, the weather, the distance, the power required to land the ball where you are asking it to land. All of this information gets transferred via hormones and energy information into the muscles of the body to produce the appropriate swing to fulfil your requested vision. Are you going to try and do this or are you going to clear your mind, enter the empty space getting out of the way in total trust? This is your only choice. When you look at this logically it is common sense that our conscious mind does not have the ability to calculate all of this information; however this is what so many golfers are doing.

The unconscious mind which gives instructions to the physical body only exists in the present moment as it has no conception of time, of past and future. It is just obediently waiting for your instructions 'in the now' to carry out the information you are you giving it.

In this example it is 'please repeat the bad shot I have just done!' At the same time you have also been giving the brain another piece of information - 'I want you to carry out this new shot.' How on earth can that inner mind perform both bits of information at the same time? It's not possible, therefore your next shot will be a combination of something you are trying to achieve and something you don't want to achieve. The result is a bad shot.

Let me give you a bit of advice, as this is a key learning tip. When you are stuck and hung up on a bad shot mentally or emotionally move away from the shot and do as many practice swings as you can before taking your new shot to discharge the incorrect energy pattern contained in the nervous system. You are then 'pulling the trigger of the gun' before you put in a new shell.

What this achieves is to release your negative emotional reaction before you take your new shot serving as it were to wipe the slate clean.

This negative information created by your thoughts is produced by you dwelling on the previous bad shot. These thoughts immediately start programming your inner mind as to what to do next. Although you do not intend to have another bad shot your mind does not know that difference. It is a bit like me asking you not to think of red. You have to think of red not to think of red!

The negative thoughts have to be released from the physical body through action before you take your next shot. This also applies to anytime that you change your mind just before taking a shot. I saw this happen with a pro player I was coaching when he changed his mind from one type of shot to another just before taking the swing. The result was a bad shot.

You will have to experiment with what works for you as an individual but whatever it is it needs to involve some physical action. Let me provide some examples that you could use. Turn around and move away form the shot, do a little dance, jump up and down, perform some sort of stretching action, find your own routine but learn this technique, learn this little trick. Discharge the mind energy information programmed in the nervous system through the physical body by movement. Performing some action will clear the nervous system from any negative programming.

You will then need to centre yourself which you will learn how to do further on in this course, how to empty your mind, be in the present moment with the attitude of 'one shot at a time'.

Dr Nariyuki Hayashi, the Japanese Neurosurgeon says that when the word 'goal' enters the mind the brain takes it as something already achieved and at that moment a top athlete's physical performance drops to the level of an average athlete. He says human brains work in a way that causes such mistakes and this can be a pitfall for athletes.

Proof of this was revealed in an experiment designed to show how the brain works when a person becomes conscious of a goal. Four university athletes exercised for one minute. During that time each student was given two different kinds of information. First they are made to think that the goal is close. The professor tells the student that he is about to reach the goal. Next the student is told that he has a long way to go. The change in brain activity in reaction to the two different types of information is measured by the amount of blood flow. When told the goal is still far off three of the four students' frontal lobe areas related to concentration and eagerness turned red due to increased blood flow. On the other hand information that a goal is near doesn't lead to a rise in brain activity.

Dr. Kikunori Shinohara from the Tokyo University of Science says that during a race or a competition parts of the brain that should be working may become less active when the racer thinks the goal is near. Making athletes think that the goal is further away than it really is helps the athletes to stay motivated and to concentrate, resulting in peak performance. With the Beijing Olympics drawing close Japanese athletes practiced hard to keep swimming without the goal in mind. This same principle applies to golf. The Japanese swimming team head coach, Norimasa Hirai said that in line with Dr Hayashi's advice he told the athletes that the race doesn't end until they touch the end, look back and check their times. In the game of golf the game is not over until the ball has entered the 18th hole. At the Olympics the Japanese gold medallist looked fully focused until he checked the board to see his world record finish. Understanding how thought affects the body is one factor behind the swimming team's great Olympic success.

The neurosurgeon, Dr Hayashi says athletes are often told to be strong and put everything into a race. But they are seldom taught how to link their mental and physical strengths. He says he has seen many capable athletes lose because they weren't fully informed about how their mind works and decided he had to do something about this.

Winter sports athletes aiming for the Vancouver Olympics are also taking advantage of neuro-scientific theories. On this day Dr Hayashi was invited to a training camp for Japan's ski-cross team. Hayashi believes ski-cross which requires both speed and technique is the kind of sport in which the mind most affects performance. Hayashi says that the moment skiers think they have made a mistake they face a losing battle. This principle also applies to the golfer.

The scientists take note of the negative words athletes often think of ahead of a crucial race. For example one Olympic skier says she tends to think of her other past poor results and starts feeling stiff. Hayashi tells her she should never think negatively, for example that she's no good or that the race will be tough. Positive thinking is the basic requirement. Hayashi told the skiers the key to victory is consciously avoiding negative words, even during training. Yes, this also applies to playing golf.

As a golfer you can fully appreciate the last thing you want to do is to have a tension, any stiffness in the body. Negative thoughts and emotions, feeling bad about yourself, are a major contributing factor for this to occur. To give an example, one of the Olympic skiers, Hiromi Takizawa says he learned that the ability to fully exert one's potential depends to a large extent on whether one knows how to control the mind.

Dr. Kenichiro Mogi, neuroscientist, has learnt that thinking about a goal is a negative idea that affects performance. Mental training is therefore crucial for athletes. The best results are achieved when the brain and body are at peak levels. Athletes need to train both their muscles and brains because the brain commands the muscles. Those aiming for Olympic gold medals need full use of their brains to make the best of their skills. In other words, the brain must be ready to perform at its peak. What is exactly meant by 'peak condition of the brain'? Until recently we could only learn from athlete's experiences of such exceptional moments which are referred to as 'flow conditions' or from the state that is also known as being 'Into the Zone'. Many athletes who set world records say that they were relaxed and just let their bodies cruise. What is happening here is that the controlling self, the ego, has let go - is out of the way, so that the total mind, the inner mind of the self takes over.

Today progress in brain imaging technology is allowing neuro-scientists to gradually see what is going on inside the brain during such peak moments. Neuroscientists are starting to see that some of the brain activities show what psychologists have talked about and what athletes have experienced for years. We can now study why some baseball batters feel that they can see the ball in slow motion. These conditions used to be beyond the scope of neuro-science which used to only focus mainly on ordinary people's brains. Scanning technology is starting to reveal new pieces of evidence.

This experience of peak performance of being 'Into the Zone' and in the flow is also experienced by many people, not just athletes. For example, think about yourself being focused on a certain task. Most people have experienced this but to exert one's ability on a big stage like that of the Olympics or a golf championship requires sports people to fully use the frontal lobe of their brains. The frontal lobe of the brain is its command centre which tells other sections of the brain what to do.

The frontal lobe includes the pre-motor cortex which controls body movements. The frontal lobes are considered our emotional control centre and home to our personality. The frontal lobes are involved in motor function, problem solving, spontaneity, memory, language, initiation, judgement, impulse control, and social and sexual behaviour.

When I say that top athletes have to be the best brain users it means that they need to learn how to train the frontal lobe. The frontal lobe controls motive and it's an area that people use in their daily lives. Top athletes have to maximise its use and science is now beginning to understand its importance.

In Los Angeles they now have a brain training gym which has contracts with more than thirty professional athletes including basket ball and soccer players. The gym focuses on athletes' brain waves. Brain waves are classified by frequency; these are delta waves, which we experience as deep sleep, theta waves which are experienced at the onset of sleep, alpha waves which are experienced as deep relaxation and beta waves which are experienced in concentration and high tension alertness.

It is the alpha state of mind which you are going to learn to achieve. It is this state of mind which will enable you to be in the flow and into the zone. The alpha state is the state of mind achieved through yoga, meditation, healing and self-hypnosis. We will discuss this state in more depth in another section of this book.

Delta waves are the slowest with beta waves being the fastest brain wave frequency. What is important for athletes are alpha waves which the brain generates when the player is relaxed together with beta waves which are produced when the player is concentrating. Contrary to most thinking being 'in the zone' all of the time is not possible. As a golfer you are going to learn to alternate the two states from the alpha state, which is 'Into the Zone' to the beta state which is a state of being focused. You will be switching between these two states.

The two states to avoid on the golf course are the theta state which is the onset of sleep and definitely avoid the delta wave state which is deep sleep, unless of course your golfing buddy is extremely boring or you are having the worst game of golf you have ever had in your life!

The brain gym provides training for athletes to keep their brain waves in the optimum state to produce good performances. Pro golfer Casey Wire has been going to the brain training gym regularly to learn how to improve his putting. In tournaments he often lost concentration and focus at crucial moments and ended up with disappointing scores. Analysis of his brain waves at the gym revealed the problem. His data contained a large blue area indicating that his brain was not generating many alpha waves. This meant that he tended to be uneasy, creating tension within his body. Casey began training to control his mental and emotional condition. He carried out various mental exercises that are contained within this course that enabled him to learn how to concentrate and produce the state of mind required for optimum performance. After twenty sessions Casey's brain scanning test results showed tremendous improvement revealing a greater section of his brain-wave patterning being in the alpha state of mind. Casey says his performance is improving as he can remember this mental condition during competitions. He says "Even if it's just for that one shot it can make a big difference, especially when playing for money. That's where it has really helped me".

In Montreal, Canada, brain training is also attracting business people. To give an example a businessman who runs a consulting firm interviews clients at length every day and finds them suitable jobs. He believes the key to success is maintaining concentration. He has begun brain training. He trains hard to improve his concentration with the help of a counsellor. After the brain training sessions he is able to go back to his consultancy job and feel that he is not as highly strung as he used to be. This has the effect of greater empathy and listening ability and his concentration skills have improved with his clients. It helps him see the whole picture, listen well to people when they talk and get every piece of information he needs to make better decisions. Particularly with today's economic situation business people would greatly benefit from training regularly.

When top athletes set records they are in a condition called 'flow'- or are 'Into the Zone'; they are concentrating but are relaxed. Tension is similar to the condition of a wild animal encountering something unknown. They enter a state of fear, their muscles tense up and they almost freeze on the spot. The objective of this course is to teach you how to concentrate, go 'into the zone' and release tension. As any golfer will tell you and I'm sure you know this to be true, it's when you tense up that your swing goes to pieces and produces a bad shot. It is through relaxed, focused concentration that you will produce the very best shot that you can physically produce.

It's quite common for people to tend to worry at crucial times that they might make mistakes. Such thoughts make them tense and unable to relax. What you are going to learn are techniques that will overcome the condition of worrying which creates tension. After learning these techniques you will be able to incorporate them in your pre-shot routine. This will create a type of inner hypnosis that will trigger the alpha state of mind bringing the body to a relaxed state. Body movements help to prepare the brain including unconscious areas, which is virtually impossible to do through will power alone.

Neuroscientists confirm this truth in their latest findings which show that deep sensations are closely connected to brain circuitry that controls emotions so by performing a gesture or other movement that makes you relax you will be able to control your tension. Deep breathing will change your state of consciousness and we have included an exercise to learn to help you easily achieve this. Learning these techniques will also flow over into creating benefit for your daily life. Synapses which connect nerve cells do not change easily. This is why it is important to regard the whole process like a drill - repetition twenty-one times minimum will bring about a new neural pathway in the brain that can be built upon.

Top swimmers for example train to remain relaxed in tense situations involving heavy pressure. Only repeated training allows them to use their brains to lead them to the podium. We all have goals to achieve in our life and try to advance step by step. How can we prepare our brains to approach our goals? First remember that relaxed concentration is the best state of mind - you don't have to be nervous about the goal.

This is what you will learn by using our first CD1 in Step 2 'The Practice - The Experience of Entering the Zone' which will teach you how to get your mind to work for you. This CD will train you how to achieve the alpha state of mind at will whenever you so desire. Repeated use of this CD1 in conjunction with learning the breathing exercise is essential to do for twenty-one days. The more times you can enter in and out of the zone the easier it will become, so repetition in this area really is the secret to your success.

A positive self image and personal ability is also another important ingredient in achieving excellence in your game of golf. Again we will discuss this in greater detail further on in the book, but a simple line to remember this by is 'we become what we think about'. The pictures in our minds create the reality in which we live, so it's really important to create a picture in our mind that we want to experience in our lives. We have included two very useful exercises to help you which you will find at the back of the book.

How the Mind Works

Creating Excellence - Achieving Your True Potential

Learning how the mind works will maximise the effectiveness of your life and this will create excellence in your game of golf. You will learn 'The Secret' of how your mind works in relation to 'The Law of Attraction'. You will also discover 'The Key' to clearing the blocks that prevent you from getting exactly what you want.

Rule No. 1   Every Thought or Idea Causes a   Physical Reaction

Your thoughts can affect all of the functions of your body. WORRY thoughts trigger changes in the stomach that in time can lead to ulcers.

ANGER thoughts stimulate your adrenal glands and the increased adrenaline in the bloodstream causes many body changes.

ANXIETY and FEAR thoughts affect your pulse rate.

Ideas that have a strong emotional content almost always reach the subconscious mind, because it is the feeling mind and the emotional body. Once accepted, these ideas continue to produce the same body reaction over and over again; they then become a repeated pattern of behaviour.

In order to eliminate or change chronic negative bodily reactions we must reach the subconscious mind and change the idea responsible for the reaction. This is easily done using meditation, inner self-awareness and autosuggestion as this creates what is known as 'The Alpha State'. It is in the alpha state that the conscious mind and the subconscious mind synchronize and become one mind. This will be learnt by using CD1 – Getting Your Mind to Work For You. It is as if the gate or barrier is lowered allowing new ideas to enter and alter existing ideas.

Rule No. 2   What is Expected Tends To Be   Realised, Your Beliefs

The brain and the nervous system respond to mental images. It is the same whether the image is self-induced or comes from the external world. The mental image formed becomes the blueprint and the subconscious mind uses every means at its disposal to carry out the plan, as presented to the inner-self in the form of an image.

A creative positive use of this rule to assist in reprogramming negative thoughts and behaviours is to use the alpha state of mind as achieved using CD1 together with the visualization of what you wish to happen.

Worrying is a form of programming a picture of what we don't want, but the subconscious mind acts to fulfil the pictured situation. It goes something like this.

"THE THINGS THAT I HAVE FEARED HAVE COME UPON ME".

Many people suffer from chronic anxiety, which is simply a subconscious mental expectancy that something terrible will happen to them (known as catastrophic expectation).

On the other hand, we all know people who seem to have that 'Magic' touch. Life seems to shower them with blessings for no apparent reason, and we call them 'Lucky'. What seems to be luck is in reality 'POSITVE MENTAL EXPECTANCY' - a strong belief that they deserve to be successful. This is because 'WE BECOME WHAT WE THINK ABOUT'.

Our physical health is largely dependent upon our mental expectancy. Physicians recognize that if the patient expects to remain sick, lame, paralyzed and helpless - even to die - the expected condition tends to be realized. The inner-self/unconscious mind dutifully carries out the ego conscious mind's request; the manifestation of an individual's desires via their own personal thought processes.

This is where meditation, self-awareness with positive visualization can become the tool to remove despondency and negative attitudes bringing about a hopeful positive expectancy - the expectancy of health, strength and well-being, which then tends to be realised.

Rule No. 3   Imagination is more powerful than Knowledge when dealing with your own Mind or the Mind of Another

This is an important rule to remember when using self-awareness with creative visualization meditation.

"REASON IS EASILY OVERRULED BY IMAGINATION"

Most of us feel superior to those who lose their savings to con men, or blindly follow a demagogue such as Hitler or are sold worthless stocks. We can easily see that such people have allowed their imagination to overcome their reason.

We are often blind to our own superstitions, prejudices and unreasonable beliefs. Any idea accompanied by a strong emotion such as anger, hatred, love, or our political and religious beliefs, usually cannot be modified through the use of reason. In using the alpha state of mind as learnt on CD1, meditation, self-awareness, we can form images in the subconscious mind - the feeling mind – the emotional body and remove, alter or amend the old ideas.

Rule No. 4 Opposing Ideas Cannot be Held at One and the Same Time

This does not mean more than one idea cannot be remembered or harboured in your memory, but it refers to the subconscious mind recognizing an idea.

Many people try to hold opposing ideas simultaneously. A man might believe in honesty and expect his children to be honest. Yet he engages daily in slightly dishonest business practices. He may try to justify these by saying: "All of my competitors do it - it's an accepted practice". However, he cannot escape the conflict and its effect upon his nervous system that is caused by trying to hold opposing ideas at the same time.

Rule No. 5 Once an Idea has been Accepted by the Subconscious it Remains until it is Replaced by another Idea

The companion rule to this is: the Longer the Idea Remains, the More Opposition there is to Replacing it with a New Idea

Once an idea has been accepted, it tends to remain. The longer it is held, the more it tends to become a fixed habit of thinking. This is how habits of action are formed, both good and bad. First there is the thought and then the action.

We have habits of thinking as well as habits of action. However the thought or idea always comes first. Hence it is obvious if we wish to change our actions we must begin by changing our thoughts.

We accept as true certain facts. For example, we accept that the sun rises in the East and sets in the West, even though the day may be cloudy and we cannot see the sun! This is a fact which governs our actions under normal conditions.

However, we have many thought habits which are not correct and yet, are fixed in the mind. Some people believe that at critical times they must have a drink of whisky or a tranquilizer or cigarette to steady their nerves so that they can perform effectively. This is not correct but the idea is there and is a fixed habit of thought. There will be opposition to replacing it with a correct idea!

To identify these rules, we are speaking of 'fixed' ideas, not just idle thoughts or passing fancies. We need to alter fixed ideas or to use them. No matter how fixed the ideas may be or how long they have remained they can be changed with self-self-awareness and the use of 'CD1 with auto-suggestion'. You can reprogramme your subconscious mind! This applies to your negative golf behaviours and unwanted swing patterns.

Rule No. 6 An Emotionally Induced Symptom Tends to Cause Organic Change if Persisted in Long Enough

It has been acknowledged by many reputable medical men that more than seventy percent of human ailments are functional rather than organic.

This means that the function of the organ or other part of the body has been disturbed by the reaction of the nervous system to negative ideas held in the subconscious mind.

This does not mean to imply that every person who complains of an ailment is emotionally ill. There are diseases caused by germs, parasites, viruses and other things attacking the human body. However, we are a single organism, the mind in the body and the two cannot be separated. Therefore, if you continue to fear ill health, constantly talk about your 'nervous stomach', 'tension headaches' or 'my aching back', in time organic changes must occur. This is a fear, anxiety based fixation upon a negative condition.

Rule No. 7   Each Suggestion Acted Upon   Creates Less Opposition to Successive Suggestion

A mental trend is easier to follow the longer it lasts unbroken. Once a habit is formed it becomes easier to follow and more difficult to break. In other words, once a self suggestion has been accepted by your subconscious mind it becomes easier for additional suggestions to be accepted and acted upon.

This is why when you are just beginning with auto suggestion, creative visualisation or self awareness in conjunction with CD1; we recommend that you start with simple suggestions. You can suggest, for instance, that you feel a warm and pleasant feeling or wish to feel and experience relaxation with focused centeredness. When these simple examples have been followed you can move to more complicated suggestions. You could for example begin with the suggestion that you would automatically awaken from self awareness or meditation in ten minutes.

Rule No. 8   When Dealing with the Subconscious Mind and its Functions 'The Greater the Conscious Effort - The Less the Subconscious Response'

This proves why 'will-power' doesn't really exist! If you have had insomnia you've learned the harder you try to go to sleep, the more wide-awake you've become. This applies to your game of golf; the harder you try for that putt the more it eludes you. You then tend to follow with some self punishing remark like 'You idiot not again you can't even putt that simple putt'. You are of course programming yourself to create a miss over and over again. The rule is when dealing with the subconscious mind, 'TAKE IT EASY'. This means you work to develop a positive mental expectancy that your problem can be and will be solved.

As your faith in your subconscious mind increases you will learn to 'let it happen' rather than trying to 'force it to happen'.

The whole purpose of providing you with these psychological and physiological truths of how the mind and body work together is to enable you to realize and become aware of your own thinking patterns. I want to give you the tools to enable you to create proof in your own life that you can change from a negative expectation and thinking pattern into a positive and creative mental expectation for your life.

The whole purpose is to allow you to obtain a mastery over your own life creating the destiny you choose to have. Once you have discovered that, you can re-program your own thinking; creating your own destiny. Then you will be ready to take the next step and that is leaping into and aligning yourself with the Universal Mind of Creation. Have fun and enjoy your swing.

'Learning to Create Your Destiny
&
Having a Positive Self Image comes first'

The Power of Imagination

What you rehearse over and over again in your mind conditions you!

Remember to use Visualisation!

How We Limit Personal Growth Unintentionally

We are constantly affecting our state by the pictures we make in our imagination and by the way we talk to ourselves, our perceptions.

Inappropriate Rules and Self-Limiting Beliefs

Use your personal improvement techniques to bring positive change to these areas, especially when you find conscious resistance.

The interesting thing is that most of us really try to live by impossible and inhuman rules and then feel guilty or angry because they exist.

Become a little bit more human! Become flexible.

For example: ALWAYS eat all the food on your plate
                NEVER rock the boat

In the beginning these rules were usually learnt to fit a special situation and were then generalized.

You can find out YOUR rules by paying attention to all your 'alwayses', 'nevers', 'shoulds' and 'oughts'. If you try to live up to them I can guarantee that you will have many experiences of failure and lots of guilty feelings about yourself plus angry feelings towards others.

How You Can Change Your Rules and Beliefs

For example, let's take a popular inappropriate rule: –

Never argue with your elders
can change to .....
I can never argue with my elders
can change to.......
I can sometimes argue with my elders
can change to......

I can sometimes argue with my elders when I have a difference
of opinion
can change to.......
I can argue with my elders when I have a difference of opinion
and when I choose to

Each of these additions represents a stage of risk and new learning. It is something that really can be lived up to.

It is your beliefs about your golf game that need to examined
and if they are self limiting or negative they will act like a command
program inside your mind to produce that very outcome in your
golf swing. For example a bad putter normally believes that they are
a bad putter. It is this belief that needs to change to 'I am a good
putter'. Use the exercise above to help create your visualisation
when using the putting CD. You may need to use this in conjunction with a technical lesson from your PGA golf professional.

We Need Guides - Not Rules

The last transformation gives you a human guide to aid you in
the human situations in which you find yourself and frees you to
make appropriate choices.

What makes it possible to enhance our feelings of self-esteem
(worth) is our willingness to be open to new possibilities, to try
them on for size, and then, if they fit us, to practice using them
until they are ours.

To start this process of being yourself there are Five Guides to live by which I learned from the wonderful family therapist Virginia Satir: -

First Guide:

The freedom to see and hear what is here,
instead of what should be, was, or will be.

Second Guide:

The freedom to say what one feels and thinks,
instead of what one should.

Third Guide:

The freedom to feel what one feels,
instead of what one ought.

Fourth Guide:

The freedom to ask for what one wants,
instead of always waiting for permission.

Fifth Guide:

The freedom to take risks on one's own behalf, instead of choosing to be only 'secure' and not rocking the boat.

What is the 'Inner Zone'?

I quite often get asked "What is this 'Inner Zone'?" I always have to say to people it is a personal experience. But have you ever looked up into the sky on a clear night in wonder and awe, seeing the moon, all the stars and the luminous radiance of the Milky Way? What is it that creates this inner feeling of wonder? What is it that decides what shot you are about to take if we know through neuroscience that you first have to decide what you are going to do and then that information is transferred from the frontal lobe of the brain to the subconscious mind which is connected to the motor nervous system creating a physical effect - simply producing a golf swing? That is science able to provide to us the mechanics of how it works and what parts of our brain and body create different functions.

What or who is it that is making these decisions? When you look into the sky at night the sky is full of bright sparkling lights and space. It is this reflection of something mysterious existing inside of you. I am unable to give a name to this inner zone; I will leave you to do this. What I can share with you is how to connect with it and as a result of this connection what effect will happen to you that will dramatically change your game of golf.

If you are not left speechless when you look up into the sky at night, you are not really looking; you have not become aware of the totality that is there. Look again and this time before you do, prepare yourself by using the abdominal breathing exercise in the back of this book.

Please do not be concerned that you are unable to have this tremendous experience of total inner freedom, it will come. Perhaps no-one has ever taught you how to experience this before now. It is never too late; just follow my guidance with sincerity and it will happen for you too. When you prepare yourself by changing your breathing, you move your consciousness from your mind, your ego, down to the centre of your being. You become free from the limitations of the conscious mind, with its associations to all the objects in your life, the psychological limitations of who you are as a human being, the constant concern about trying to control your existence and everything that you own, your material and emotional possessions.

It is no wonder unhappiness is experienced by so many people on the planet today. The more we have, the more we try to hold on to what we have amassed. The true reality of our existence can be explained by quantum physics which shows that everything in existence is unstable as it is constantly changing. This includes everything that appears to be fixed, things, events, experiences are in a constant state of flux, therefore it's inevitable that change will occur and if we become dependent upon those illusionary fixed things that we have now as a source of our happiness and existence we are also going to meet disaster and unhappiness because those things that we have now will change.

Quantum physics has revealed that our whole existence, the galaxies, the universe, all of life comes from an empty space, something that they call the unified field and this unified field is non-changing in nature, so from the space of nothingness all existence comes into form. It is constantly changing the shape of its form through our interaction of thought which bring into existence through the law of attraction our material experience. You are like a potter with a lump of clay who moulds it into a shape. Your life is like this - your thoughts are what shape your existence. This mysterious space is conscious and I can share with you that it is a source of pure joy and personal security when you are aware of its existence. Tom Watson from the USA on day three of the 2009 Open at Turnbury, Scotland had an incredible round of golf putting him into the lead for the final fourth day, with everyone expecting him to walk away with the claret cup trophy. When interviewed about his amazing performance his main reply was the state of Serenity he was experiencing throughout the round that carried him round the course with ease. This is the effect of this mystical inner state we are calling the inner zone.

'Into the Zone' is about connecting with this inner space within you. The awe you experience when looking at the sky at night can be experienced within you. The first CD1 in this course teaches you how to get 'Into the Zone' so that you too can benefit from this birthright source of inner resource. At this stage I will not go into this further as this skill is all you need to master for you to achieve excellence and the joy of golf within your own life. If, however, you would like to discover more about this subject you can find this in our spiritual section within the book 'The Seekers Guide for a New Awakening' which contains essential teachings for your spiritual enlightenment. Although this may appear completely non-related to mastering the inner realm of golf there is one course contained within that book entitled 'The Excellent You' which expands upon creating excellence in your own life. You may be interested in our MP3 download version of this course, again available from our website at www.new-awakening.co.uk.

Another experience that automatically happens for some people is that they awaken to their ability to heal themselves. If this happens to you apart from the benefit of rejuvenation, yes, many people start looking younger as a result of this discovery, you will find the ability to heal of great benefit for physical wellbeing, healing sports injuries. If you do awaken to this gift we have created a multimedia course to teach you more entitled 'Reiki Healing First Degree'. Again you will discover this on our New Awakening website www.new-awakening.co.uk.

When you change on the inside
the outside changes naturally without willpower

This statement is a key statement to embrace in this new way of thinking. Why is this? Simply it enables you to take responsibility for your life as a creator, as opposed to being a victim of life's circumstances, those things that are happening outside of you which you have no control over.

The feeling of awe comes from the depth of space that contains the multitude of galaxies held within and given birth from it. When you become aware of this space, the mystical indefinable nature that

What is the 'Inner Zone'?

'IS', your being becomes filled with a new awareness. It is this awareness that fills you with joy, fills you with a depth that is immeasurable. Accept that you have now gone beyond the small sphere of your mind, your ego, your conditioned life. It is this pure awareness that will bring you a clear mind, a focused mind, an undisturbed mind. It is this state of mind that you need to achieve before you can create your inner game of golf from within the zone. This is why I focus with great emphasis on the importance of mastering the first CD1, the ability to enter the zone. So this will be your first goal - achieving the state of awareness as this is getting 'into the zone'. This course has two audio sections; CD1 teaches you how to get into the zone. The second part of the course CD2 to CD5 will teach you what to do when you have achieved this state of mind; how to play the game of golf with new creative awareness for your long game, your short game, for your putting and how to play in competitions being emotionally centred.

I have been helping people successfully achieve this amazing state of awareness for over 25 years and this is what I am now sharing with you. One fact that is important for you to appreciate is that without a change of awareness nothing will change in your inner game. You may read many books on golf psychology, attend seminars, enter phone coaching, all of these ways are helpful for your conscious mind to think in a different way but without the deep inner connection that you are now going to be learning by using our first CD1, 'Getting your Mind to Work for You - Teaching you How to Get 'Into the Zone' nothing much will happen.

It was Einstein who said "You can't change a problem or a situation with the same mind that created it". What he meant by this was very simply you have to enter a higher state of awareness than your normal mind state and then in a mysterious way the problems quite often change of their own accord, they disappear; they dissolve into this greater awareness.

He was quite brilliant to realise that our mind is what has created our problems and limitations, therefore if we try and use the same mind to try and solve the problem it will be impossible. Only from a different awareness will you be able to bring a new perspective to the problem, in fact what I have discovered is that the problem changes by itself without doing anything. It is as if the shift in your awareness brings a larger view to the situation, putting it into perspective causing the limitation, the limited perspective to dissolve.

The Law of Attraction states 'What we put our attention on will come into our lives', as if our thoughts are magnetic or we are placing our order to the universe which dutifully responds and fulfils our request, bringing into our lives the very thing or experience we have desired. Yes, what we think really does create our lives.

So what stops us from getting everything we desire is contained in the beliefs we hold. It is through bringing new awareness, by entering 'Into the Zone' to any situation which brings about a change automatically, effortlessly. This new approach will astound you. Who is this new you, this amazingly clear minded emotionally centred golfer you will become?

What I am saying is take your time, master step one by practicing going 'Into the Zone' for twenty-one days. When you feel refreshed having a new awareness and realisation as a result of practicing with this CD1 then you can move on to step two, creating your game from your own inner space.

In reality you cannot see space of course, you can't touch, smell or hear it, so how do you know it exists? There is something within you that can relate with space; this is why you can become aware of it. In some way you know it although the senses you use to experience the outer world are unable to know it. So when you look at the sky at night the eye cannot see the space, this no-thing, but inside you there is a knowing in your heart, you intuitively know it. It is a heartfelt experience.

When you are aware of space you are really only aware of 'awareness itself' the inner space of consciousness. This formless consciousness that lies behind our perception makes all experience possible as it is no longer obscured by form. It is this space, this formless space, this creative universal aspect where you will bring into existence form and in your personal interest, your perfect swing. It is this resource within you that creates an expanded awareness within your mind.

It is in this inner zone that you will learn to play your inner game of golf. Am I being cruel by taking you to the end at the beginning? As you read this book this concept will become clearer as your mind desperately needs to make meaning from what is being presented. In reality the concept that all comes from the highest state of awareness that exists in the cosmos can only be understood when it is experienced. Therefore please do not be concerned if you do not understand what I am trying to share as this is a common experience. I quite often receive statements from people saying things like "You must be crazy, life is not that simple, what are you on?"

The very same people after trying what I am offering once they have had the experience of the inner zone have returned to me in great joy sharing "I now understand, I now know what you were trying to share with me". But what I am trying to share cannot be conveyed in words, only through experience so please throw yourself into this wholeheartedly, experiment with this conscious- ness for yourself.

Most books are written with a very long lead up to the final revelation made in the near to last chapter. I am different; I respect your time. You want to know the key to getting 'Into the Zone' so I am sharing this at the beginning. The explanations will follow as you read on; you will also need to know what to do when you have experienced this state of being; how to create from within the inner zone – use CDs 2-5 for this purpose.

Please enjoy this course keeping an open mind, free from judgement. Try what I suggest before you dismiss it. I deeply appreciate your life and know you probably know more about golf than I do, however when it comes to the mind and how it works trust me, I have discovered its secrets as this has been my life's study and practice and it's these secrets which I wish to share with you. The good news is that they are very easy to learn. Allow me to share with you the shortcuts that can take you within twenty-one days to achieve the inner state of mind every golfer dreams about and some top professionals have learnt to do.

Many people are only partly living as they have not fully experienced this inner space quality at will. People normally are so caught up with the personal identity, their own thoughts and emotions experiencing life only through the five senses where life is coming into them from the outside, that they have disconnected themselves from the creative source of their existence that is lying hidden and dormant within their own inner zone.

You are going to discover the goldmine that you have been sitting on all of your life. It's a little bit like the story of the man who was desperately in need of wealth. Travelling in search of this wealth he came across an old chest. He sat down for a rest, looked out all around him and said "I'm never going to find this fortune I am seeking". If he had only considered looking inside the chest he was sitting on he would have realised it was full of gold bars. He would have become a multi-millionaire.

Not only will your golf improve but your life will change more positively, attracting better situations and experiences into your life. This will occur as a result of unlocking the doors to your own inner paradise, your very own inner goldmine and your perfect game of golf.

Space - Expanded Consciousness

You can participate in the dance of creation and become active without attachment to outcome, without placing unreasonable demands upon the world that is constantly changing in its unstable construction. Are you looking outside of yourself into the world asking the world "Fulfil me, make me happy, make me safe, tell me who I am"? In reality the world cannot give you these things and when you no longer have such expectations all self-created suffering comes to an end. All such suffering is due to an over valuation of form and personal goals, resulting from an unawareness of the dimension of inner space. When that dimension is present in your life you can enjoy things, experiences and the pleasure of the senses without losing yourself in them, without inner attachment to them, that is to say, without being addicted to the world.

When the dimension of space is lost or rather not known, which is true for a lot of people, the things of the world assume an absolute importance, a seriousness and heaviness that in truth they do not have.

Being Present

Awareness implies that you are not only conscious of things (objects) but you are also conscious of being conscious. If you can sense an alert inner stillness in the background while things happen in the foreground - that's it! This inner dimension is there in everyone and in everything but most people are completely unaware of it.

Ask yourself this "Can you feel your own presence?" Whenever you are upset about an event, a person or a situation the real cause is not the event, person or situation but a loss of true perspective that only space can provide. You are trapped in object consciousness, unaware of the timeless inner space of consciousness itself. The words 'This too will pass' when used as a pointer can restore awareness of that dimension to you.

This point is specifically relevant to playing golf; you become attached to the object, the outcome, which in reality you have no control over whatsoever and then you suffer because it's not going your way. You know the suffering causes tension, anxiety, and you know the beginning of this circle, this cycle is a tense body that produces a bad shot.

The solution is to relinquish your attachment to outcome. This will be your challenge and it's a big one, but it's the only one that makes sense and it's the only one that truly works. To quote a great English golfer Paul Cassidy in the BMW PGA Championship at Wentworth Golf Club, Virginia Water, Surrey on the second day when interviewed and asked how he was getting on, he was not concerned about the scores whatsoever and said "I'm just having fun. I'm not worrying about the swing at all". What was he doing? We can all learn from this attitude because what he was doing was staying within the present moment, not being concerned about the statistics, the results; he was playing his golf and many of you may know at this period of his life he was having problems with his back swing. He let go of that completely and entered into 'the now' and was playing his game of golf like a beginner who had discovered the thrill of hitting the ball for the first time. This amazing championship was being experienced as a joyful occasion.

Being In The Present Moment

Presence is a state of inner spaciousness. When you are in the present you ask "How do I respond to the needs of this situation, of this moment?" In fact, you don't even need to ask the question; you are still, alert, open to what is. You bring a new dimension into the situation and that dimension is space. You look and you listen thus you have become one with the situation.

When instead of reacting against the situation you merge with it the solution arises out of the situation itself. Actually, it is not you, the person, who is looking and listening but it is stillness itself. Then if action is possible or necessary you take action without thinking. A confident knowingness arises from within the zone, the inner space, then right action happens through you. The ball and target have become one. Right action is appropriate to the whole. When the action is accomplished the alert, spacious stillness remains.

This will become your guide; the barometer you use that lets you know if you have taken action based upon your limited mind and conditioning or if the action which in this case is your swing is coming from within the zone.

All creativity and freedom comes out of this inner spaciousness. Once you have taken your swing from within the zone your ball is moving towards its intended target. Your task is to remain vigilant so the notion of 'me' or 'mine' does not arise. If you take total credit for what you have accomplished the ego has returned and the spontaneous has been obscured.

What is happening is the inner zone will close and your old mind and emotions will revert back to the limitations of their conditioning. In fact your consciousness will have contracted again. You will have fallen back into the trap of the ego's limitations once again.

I am not suggesting you don't enjoy the pleasure and joy that the effortless shot has just provided you; the joy and pleasure is part of the reward, is part of the experience. What I am suggesting is that as this happens, as you enjoy this moment, that you maintain an attitude of gratitude, acknowledging that you on your own have not created this, giving credence to the part the inner zone has played in the oneness of mind/body co-ordination in the oneness of ball and target phenomena.

To say this another way, by not acknowledging the part the inner zone has played, the ego and personality taking total credit, is like drawing the curtains on a window closing out the sun. The ball and the target exist in a different time space in a different location. From the limited senses of the self you see two places. From the realm of the inner zone of inner space there is no separation; they become one. This technique and understanding has been used for centuries by Zen Buddhist archers, Shaolin monks and the like. They understand that to hit the target they have to become one with it and this is what you are going to learn to do once you have mastered connection with the zone. You are then going to learn how to become one with the club, with the ball and with the target. This is how your future golf game will be played; from within the inner zone; you are now in flow.

Your success as a golfer will contain three ingredients to create a three-fold approach. One is your technical ability. Two is your physical ability with your core stability and the third is your mental ability.

At the end of each round of golf and not during your round of golf you can assess these three areas and give yourself a self-help plan of what you need to do to improve upon where you are. This might mean going to the golf pro and taking more lessons in a specific area of your game which might be putting, chipping or some aspect with your swing. I feel in the technical part of the game it is essential to maintain regular lessons and every golf club has tremendous resource in its coaching staff and the courses they run.

The evidence in neuroscience today shows that repeated behaviour becomes a learnt memory. Therefore if you just rely upon teaching yourself without professional tuition you will ingrain negative swing patterns. I'm sure you know golfers or maybe even yourself who have been self-taught and learnt bad habits. This will normally create ingrained patterns which become difficult to change and of course these patterns are limiting your game of golf.

The good news is that if you start taking lessons now and I recommend you do in conjunction with going 'Into the Zone' and retraining your brain you will be able to replace these bad habits, these bad swing patterns that are contained within your own inner memory. So this course works very, very well in partnership with the teaching professional.

Going beyond the voice in your head!

What does this mean and why is this so important? When you are possessed by the voice in your head your perceptions and experiences are distorted by instant judgements that cover and cloud the opportunity of experiencing 'what is happening at this very precise moment'. The voice in the mind creates a block from the truth of what is in the now.

Most people are experiencing some past event that is trying to repeat itself again which is obviously based upon a past memory. As a golfer it is very important for you to understand how your mind works because of the repeated process of making a golf swing. The golf swing can easily become a slippery slope of ingrained negative thought patterns which translate into negative bodily actions of limitations. These in turn then result in self-punishment with feelings of inadequacy, producing repeated unhealthy nervous reactions to certain places and situations on the golf course or within competitive play. This is a downward spiral beset with unhappy feelings, disappointment and dissatisfaction.

When you understand how the mind works you can then drive the car instead of being on negative auto-pilot and having no control over your outcomes whatsoever, in fact becoming power-less at the mercy of a negative conditioned inner mind memory.

What you are going to learn is how to overcome and recondition the mind to create a positive mind with positive expectation basing your awareness in the only reality that is important for you 'in the now'.

Translating this concept into golf it is the ball you are about to hit. This is the only shot that exists. You have no past feelings to compare with what you are about to experience. The shot has not yet happened so how can you have any feelings about it based upon your past experience?

The solution to this negative cycle, this negative talking, this negative internal dialogue is your ability to master 'entering the zone' for it is this inner zone that will fill you with confidence and will provide you with tremendous freedom, providing new possibilities, new outcomes that occur naturally all by themselves. Once again the solution remains the same - it is the mastery of our first CD1 'Entering the Zone'.

If you suffer from negative internal dialogue, talking to yourself negatively, reprimanding yourself like a schoolmaster over a naughty child, beating yourself up at every opportunity because you are feeling unworthy and in need of punishment we have provided an exercise at the back of the book that you can practice to change this unhealthy situation.

Playing 'The Inner Game of Golf'

This chapter will prepare you to become inwardly creative with your long game, chipping and your putting. The accompanying CDs listed below work together with the knowledge you already have plus the knowledge contained in this book. This wonderful combination will produce 'The Result'; this is the new experience you wish to have on the golf course. The four CDs to achieve this are: CD2 – 'The Long Game'; CD3 – 'The Short Game'; CD4 – 'Perfect Putting' and CD5 'Excel in Tournaments and Competitions'. (Note CD4 – Perfect Putting also relates to the Chapter named Putting and CD5 has its own chapter named 'Competitions with the Pros').

The information in this chapter will help you produce a result that creates effortless golf through mastering the inner game. When you go into the zone you have to first load your conscious mind with information that you wish your unconscious mind to create for you, the type of result you wish to produce on the golf course. For this reason I have included some basics about the golf game so that you can have a reference in your mind when you create the shot in your imagination using visualisation. This comes after you have mastered going into the zone. This chapter is all about what to practice using the CDs 2-5 when you are 'in the zone' at home, which will prepare and condition you before you go onto the golf course. This is all about practice and preparation for training your mind to work for you.

Key points to include when
Creating Your Inner Game of Golf

The golf swing has to change in the brain first to train your mind for golf

- You must be prepared to change your habits
- Develop a new routine
- Be patient – the results will come
- Only ever work on one thing at a time
- Practising your technique or
- Simulating game conditions

Visualisation and Picturing what you want

How to visualise the shot in your inner mind's eye; this will create whole mind awareness, producing holistic mind-body coordination at ease.

Get the Fun back into your game today and stop beating yourself up on the golf course.

When you review your shot focus on what you did well!

Every shot you make will have positive and negative aspects to it. Your objective is to Focus on the positive aspects.

Focus on the Positive

Positive feelings create a relaxed body. A relaxed body creates the opportunity of your next shot being a Good One!

Tossing the Ball in the air to create inner focus

Tossing the ball in the air and then catching it again several times creates an inner focus which has a hypnotic effect. This can have the effect of overcoming tee-off nerves from the first tee. What is happening is that you have to give your attention to some action, to focus on the ball draws your attention away from people on the golf course or spectators at the first tee.

Let go of negative talking to yourself
or others on the course

A negative mind creates another negative shot! To focus on the negative aspects is an order to your unconscious mind to re create what you are presenting it with. For example into the bunker as a result of the hook on your last shot or fear of the water before the shot. What your conscious mind is doing is to give your unconscious mind the instructions for your next shot. The unconscious mind obeys your wishes obediently and as it controls all your physical body's muscles etc. it makes the appropriate adjustments to give you exactly what you have asked for!

Embracing acceptance is the key to happiness
The 'So What' Attitude

There is a well known fact about most golf players and that is as you continue to play over a few years, based upon your score alone, you will not realise your own progress. The reality of golf is that you continually improve and will then have a spell when you appear to go backwards and not play as well. I like to compare this to a pendulum or a golf swing.

Your mental attitude during this apparent regression to maintain your happiness and enjoyment of the game is to embrace acceptance.

In reality you have two possible approaches to this reality:

a)   Accept it and then you will maintain a relaxed mind and body. And a relaxed mind and body allows for the next good shot!

b)   Beat yourself up again because you have lost it. You can't play any more. When this happens you are in judgement of your past and only selecting your best performance and are measuring the now against that time, that past experience. You have now set yourself too high an expectation and will not be able to live up to the best game of the past. The past is dead! It is only a dream. The future also does not exist! The only reality you have is the now. In the now exists unlimited potential. Let go of the past and live in the now. Do not measure your now against your past.

The key to your success and happiness as a golfer is learning how to go into the zone, into this very now moment where no past or future exist and this is what you are going to learn. This is what all great sports people have discovered – how to create excellence in their performance.

Every player and lover of golf encounters in his experiences the same issues in respect to mastering their mind. High or low handicap makes no difference in this area; no matter what level of ability you may have from being a complete beginner to a PGA Pro player, learning to master your mind, going into the zone and drawing on untapped energy and abilities that lay within you is the secret to becoming an excellent golfer.

Example of a positive approach

The situation: the shot goes into the bunker
Positive response: "I can now practice my sand shots. Bunkers are a good opportunity to practice getting out of the sand."

Avoid comparing yourself against other golfers. This is only bound to lead to personal disappointment and negative feelings or feelings of inadequacy.

Positive attitudes

Every golf player's game fluctuates. A player will go through a good spell and also a slump; a time when nothing goes as expected. When you compare yourself to others there will always be a player who can outplay you in every aspect of your game – they can drive further, they can chip more accurately, they can control the ball with ease, what a long putt they can make! What happens when you do this is that you have lost focus on your own game; you are creating the tension of comparison causing you to lose your own personal effectiveness and personal power. One thing is for certain – the joy disappears. The black cloud appears.

The other thing that happens is that you will beat yourself up again causing feelings of helplessness and despair, even anger and frustration.

Avoid Comparisons - Remember 'The Perfect Shot' to bring back the fun into your game.

You are a perfect golfer although you don't think you are! All golfers want to enjoy their game and they want to become the best they can be. The good news for you is that every golfer is a perfect golfer because every golfer has played the perfect shot. What is this shot? It is the shot you play when the ball leaves the clubface and goes into the hole!

Yes, from The PGA champion to the beginner we are all equal because we have all made this perfect shot.

You could say 'What would be the perfect round of golf?' The answer to this would be to play a round of golf in 18 strokes! Yes, this is the only perfect round of golf and since no one has achieved this there is no such thing as a perfect round of golf. There is only the perfect stroke and that stroke is the one you make when the ball goes down the hole.

When you look at golf from this viewpoint you can have a shift in awareness within your mind, your attitude changes from frustration and comparison to acceptance and enjoyment. You now have the knowledge that when you play each hole you will have the perfect stroke at some time or another. This new attitude will create a relaxed mind and a relaxed mind will create a relaxed body and as any pro golf teacher will tell you a relaxed body is the key to a great swing.

Review to create a positive attitude

- Never compare yourself with another golfer.
- Look for the positive in every shot you make.
- You are a good golfer now!
- Whatever level of golf you are at accept it with an attitude of excitement, knowing there is so much more that you can learn.
- The game of golf can never be mastered therefore you can never get bored.
- The only perfect shot is the one that goes down the hole and not the mechanics of the stroke!

Stages of learning golf

When you use CDs 2-5 you will be using creative visualisation form within the zone. This means you will mentally prepare what you wish to happen on the golf course. The first step you need to do is prepare your mind with all the aspects of your game in a form of a movie or feeling imagination before going into the zone to program your unconscious with your new game of golf. You will create a new movie for each CD before going into the zone to re program your unconscious mind.

The key to this being successful is to do this in manageable chunks. When you have achieved small victories you will find this easier and easier to do. Before any shot on the course there are many aspects you take into account without thinking. This includes your pre shot routine. You are now going to familiarise yourself with as many golfing practical considerations you will need to learn or review to take your golf to the top of your ability.

First of all I have listed many possible considerations that you can use when you create your movie for the long game, chipping and putting. I have also included many points that will help you develop an attitude of grace; it is this attitude that maintains a connection with the inner zone.

Read these chapters repeatedly as the points will enter your subconscious mind and start affecting you in a positive way. They will also reinforce those great aspects you already have and deepen their positive effects within your game and on the course.

The fundamentals of golf - Draw on aspects of these points when you make your inner mind movie.

The first thing you need to learn is your setup, addressing the ball and the golf swing. This is purely a physical process which is best to be taught by a professional golf coach.

Cause and effect

To progress in golf after learning the fundamentals, every golf player needs to learn how to control the golf ball, how to hit better shots. You will then be on your way to lower scores.

There are four aspects to this and they are:
1. Distance
2. Direction
3. Curve
4. Height and flight – trajectory

You've picked out your target and pictured your shot. You need to be consumed with the target. Zero into it. The key here is that you are focusing your mind, your attention on the target and that is about going forwards and not backwards. You need to Think Forwards. When many golfers are learning golf they get very caught up with the backswing and this becomes a habit which they carry forward throughout their whole golfing experience. You need to change your thinking to one where you forget completely the backswing and you just focus on going forwards. A way to help you remember this is that you don't hit the ball going backwards; you are going to hit the ball going forwards.

Distance and direction

Remember, maximum force equals maximum distance. Half the force applied at the club head equals half the distance. It is not the length of the swing but it is applying the right force to obtain the right distance. The force is in the handle of the club and it is nothing to do with the club head speed. You will need to develop a oneness state of mind and body and target.

- Applied force will equal the distance the ball travels.
- Right arm extension equals the direction.
- Extend your right arm to the target because the right arm controls the direction of the shot.

Curve

The difference between a fade and a slice or a draw and a hook is dependent upon using the forearms with the hands square at the point of impact returning the clubface to the same point of address. The hands have to be square at the point of impact.

The slice is caused because the right hand has gone underneath the left hand at the point of impact, opening the club face and putting spin on the left hand side of the ball causing a large curve to the right. The hook is caused because the right hand has come over the top of the left hand at the point of impact, causing the club face to hit the ball on the right hand side producing right hand spin and curve.

The professional shot, of course, is the draw and the fade because they are intended. These are produced by keeping the hands square at the point of impact and just adjusting the club face either to the left or to the right.

- The fade = An open club face causes left to right curve
- The draw = A closed club face causes right to left curve
- Fade and draw = forearms, square hands and club face
- Hook and slice = right hand on top or underneath left hand at impact

Height and flight – Trajectory

This is brought about by the club choice plus touching the ground beyond the ball after the strike. Contact is made on the downswing and the divot is just beyond the ball.

Using visualisation and your imagination
Picturing the shot

Combine all four characteristics of cause and effect into the shot i.e. the distance, the direction, the curve and the height. You are going to visualise the ball in flight; rehearse this picture or movie in your mind before you take the shot. Imagine the ball in flight. To practice this you can then swing the golf handle and knock the tee over without a ball being there. Just swing the club from left to right. Hinge the club up and down from the wrists.

Picture the shot in your imagination doing exactly what you want. Step up to the ball and swing the handle of the club like a magic wand and just create it.

Intention is also another key

When you picture the shot you see the target, where the ball will be after you have swung the handle of the club. When you aim at the target in your mind you intend the ball to end at a certain place. This is what is happening; you gather the energy from within side yourself. You access a place of boundless energy and you sight the target. The might of the universe is now unleashed behind your vision. Even if you do not accomplish your intention you have released a powerful force into motion.

Some Days they Go and Some Days they Don't!

Your Attitude will effect your enjoyment and development of the Game.

The correct positive mental attitude to have, for each shot you make:

1. After the shot, no matter what the outcome, remain centred and emotionally calm. You can use your deep breathing or your ability to enter the zone. If your emotions are negative do not worry 'this will pass' but walk away from the next shot and discharge the negative energy that has gone into the inner mind and nervous system by taking some action.

2.   Select and review only what is positive about the shot.

3.   Regard the shot as a lesson where you will learn from the shot what will benefit the next shot you will make.

Release Inner Tension!
Release inner tension in your setup and swing

Every joint in your body should be perfectly free when you address the ball. The body consists of a system of joints and muscles. There is an energy system that runs through the body that sends information to the muscles as to how they are to behave.

The perfect swing requires that all joints in your body should be free. This means that the fingers and knuckles in your hands, your wrists, your elbows, your shoulders, the vertebrae in your back, your hips, knees, ankles and toes, even your jaw should be totally relaxed.

The problem you have is when you get tense you are sending a signal from your unconscious to all of your body to lock up. It is the same response that comes from fear, your body becomes paralysed, and the joints lock up. When the joints are locked up you cannot swing the club!

The muscles are different in that they act like a collection of rubber bands that stretch and release, contracting and releasing. They are controlled by your energy system which sends information to them through your nervous system. The central control of information comes from your unconscious mind as it responds to situations automatically, biochemically. This is what happens when you hear the known concept of, 'grooving in your swing' when you are learning a new aspect of your game. It is referring to the memory of the muscles that are to be programmed into your automatic responses to a given situation. In this case you want a bodily response to happen when you swing the club and hit the ball.

It is in this area of golf that you are learning how to make changes to your inner programming. It makes sense to me and I'm sure you will agree that if you want to change an automatic response that is not working for you, you need to change the programme that is running it. By trying to change the programme from the outside it will be difficult. This is because of the way the mind and body work as a unit. So the first thing to do is to learn how your mind works and how you can take control of your mind to reprogramme yourself to create the bodily response that will in turn produce the most brilliant golf swing for you as an individual.

Shot-making procedure – Picturing the shot

When you use your inner mind, when you know how to get into the inner zone you are able to transfer your desired shot outcome with greater effectiveness than using your conscious mind alone. By becoming aware of your inner mind you will be able to create the maximum positive effect with your golf shot. When you approach a shot you will be considering all of the environmental ingredients before you hit the ball; you will consider where the ball is in relation to where you want the ball to go, your target. Your mind will have to consider the following for your shot: how the ball lies and how we treat it, we select our target in the distance, you will picture what you want with club selection and finally you will consider your set up and the swing needed keeping your eye on the ball with the target in your inner mind's eye.

1. Pre shot routine
2. Set up needs to be consistent
3. Visualise the Target

You will need to be comfortable and consistent as this will determine how effective you are.

The Key

When you select your target your eyes will take in a lot of information i.e. the distance, the lay of the course – is it uphill or downhill, the lay of the fairway, any obstacles in the way, bunkers, water hazards, trees etc., the wind strength and the direction you want your ball to go. Your unconscious mind will search your past experience to understand how best to deal with the shot.

The Mind Set Up

The mind set up is in reverse of the action you are going to make.

1.   Picture the ball going through the air exactly as you want it to, going from where the ball is flying through the air to where you want it to land.

2.   All of the information is contained in the swing of the golf club handle.

3.   Your body will now automatically make the best swing for you.

The reason you picture the outcome of the shot in your mind is because you will programme and encode the energy that will be sent to your muscles to produce the perfect swing for you. You can now believe this because of the evidence provided in neuroscience.

What happens when we talk about becoming aware of negative programming, e.g. fear of the bunker, the water hazard, the memory of a negative past shot? Your mind is selecting the negative aspects of the shot you have just made or are about to make and loading them in the frontal lobe of the mind. The inner mind is now encoding messages that get communicated to the body to produce what you are thinking about. If you focus on the negative shot you are asking your mind to produce it for you. In the case of focusing on the obstacle i.e. the water hazard the mind now takes that to be the target as it contains the strongest message it receives as it normally is very emotionally charged. You take your shot and your body produces the shot towards the target, yes your ball ends up in the water hazard or the bunker.

When you understand how the process works you will understand why your shot behaved as it did. You programmed your body by your thoughts; you gave your body instructions as to what you wanted it to do. The amazing thing is that you produced the shot, although in the case of negative thinking or programming you are baffled by the outcome. "Oh no, not again" you will say to yourself. Just take a moment and consider what will happen when you program your mind with positive thoughts. Yes you will get positive shots; your body will produce the best shot it can to create the outcome you have asked for. This will be just beyond the restrictions of your physical and technical ability.

An Overview

Mind set on the target - you picture the shot you are going to make in your inner mind. This programmes your unconscious mind with what messages to send biochemically, created by the hypothalamus in the brain, to the muscles in your body to produce the shot pictured in your mind.

Become positive, relaxed and enjoy your game

Four Ingredients

1. Lie of the ball
2. The target
3. You picture the shot, the inner mind message
4. Swing the golf club positively relative to the pictured shot in your mind.

You will make some human error, accept this. The physical aspects of the game need to be learned. Have lessons with your club Pro. They are essential to you becoming the best golfer you can become in conjunction with mastering your own mind and learning to play the inner game of golf.

Your swing thought can be reduced to one single thought and that is contained in the handle of the club. All the elements of the swing, the distance, the curve, the power or force, the height and the direction are all contained in the swing of the golf club handle.

Make it simple
Reduce the swing thought to one thought

You are going to swing the handle of the golf club in relation to the pictured shot in flight you have seen in your mind which relates to the point where the ball lies to where the ball will stop, your target.

From within your mind to the action of your body, from where the ball lies to the flight through the air to its destination, the target, you are going to learn how to become one. There is a connection where there is no time, no separation because your mind is one with the target, the place your ball will land.

Setting Goals and Your Game Plan
One Shot at a Time

1.   Short time goals are about staying in the present by taking each shot at a time, moving the ball from a to b.

2.   Medium range goals are to relate to par as best you can. You have to forget completely about the reward you are setting yourself as this can only lead to disappointment. Take one shot at a time, stay in the present and just relate to par; par is your opponent.

3.   How do you set your goal in relation to the match – the full 18 holes? Very simple. You take the same approach as the short and medium range goals as set out in 1 and 2 above.

A massive teaching point in relation to remaining a happy golfer – bringing joy back into your game: The reward in golf should not be pre-set but should be as a result of what happens.

Staying in the Present Moment

When you tee off you should just be focused on the shot and the hole you are playing relative to par. It is a mistake to be concerned about how many shots it takes you to hole the ball. You are only concerned about making the best shot you can which moves on to the next shot until the ball goes into the hole. This is the way to play like a Pro and to avoid a preset outcome of expectancy. This attitude will lead to a more even game producing rewards and joy as you play. For example, if you play 3 on a par 4, your reward is making a birdie, but you do not set your goal as a birdie. If you do and do not make the birdie and play a bogey, 5 on a par 4 you will feel such frustration and disappointment. I'm sure you know what I'm talking about; we have all been there. This will lead to negative mind programming which will result in more negative shots.

Your attitude and desire to be better than other golfers, better than you played before will remove you from the present moment. When you do this you remove yourself from remaining relaxed and just create tension which creates a bad swing and a bad swing as you know produces a bad shot. The solution therefore is to stay in the present moment with no attachment to outcome, able then to remain relaxed with your perfect set up to make a great shot for you as an individual. It will be the future which steals your energy into expectations, comparisons or competitiveness with other players. You will be setting yourself up for failure for the very simple reason you do not have control of all the variables that can happen in a round of golf.

Become absorbed in that which you have control of and that is your own game – your own swing. Lose sight of what your score is and then the end results happen of their own accord. Move your focus from the reward, the score, counting up the points and focus on your new goal which is to be absorbed in the present moment and just taking one shot at a time.

You don't win by trying to win!

Turn your attention inward like some top athletes have learnt to do and enter into the zone, an inner trance-like Buddhist Zen state.

Develop a "so what" attitude towards your play. Create an even emotional response to your shots and to the holes you have played. Don't get emotionally too high or too low, for if you do there is a tendency for a bad shot to follow. I have experienced this so many times on the course where I have been so delighted with my last shot that my next shot is absolutely lousy or I have been so disappointed with my last shot and obsessed with it and absorbed in it which is the past because in truth it is over, finished with and I can't let go of it. I go to take my next shot in an upset state and guess what happens; yes you've got it – another lousy shot! I'm sure you understand what I'm talking about. So the solution to this is 'do not judge the shot you have just made'. Again, you do not win by trying to win. You do have to be realistic in terms of being aware of how you are playing. Take that with you after your 18 holes and establish what you need to practice to improve. Become aware of how your mental attitude is and create the right mental attitude in playing the inner game. Stay in the present moment, play one shot at a time and just swing the club.

Do not allow your mind or your body to drift towards the things you cannot control. The psychology of competition play when you play match play compared to stroke play tends to lead to a lower overall score. This is very interesting and the reason why this occurs is because you only have to focus on one hole at a time.

Rhythm and Timing

The swing can be as fast or as slow as you want it to be, it all depends on your personality. There is a very good drill for this which you may know: swing the club back as fast as you like then at the top of the back swing say the word "set" and then like a pendulum allow the club to release and at the bottom of the swing just before you hit the ball say "swing".

Focus your attention on the speed of the club where it hits the ball. The teaching aspect of this is to put your attention on the ball area. It is known in quantum physics that attention energises which will create force and power for the stroke.

This drill and focused awareness will bring a new sense of control where you are in the swing. It also brings greater consistency. Vary the tempo to suit your personality always keeping the focus on your tempo.

(Visualisation) In your mind's eye see your club face hitting and connecting with the turf just beyond the ball. Your subconscious now knows where to connect with the ball.

To create a draw or a fade add into your visualisation the club face being slightly open or closed, connecting with the ball on the left or right side. Ask your subconscious to create the tempo or speed that best suits you as an individual; to create the shot you want to produce.

Build into your visualisation the direction of your shot. To do this see your right arm extending towards the target.

To gain an additional 20% extra distance you will need excellent co-ordination between the top of your body and your legs. For this extra distance you need to keep your weight on your back leg and move it into your right leg as you swing.

Club Selection

Whatever club you think is the right club is the right club selection for the shot. The key to this being true is in the words 'whatever club you think is the right club'. This again confirms the transference of confidence and belief to the inner mind. The inner mind will send the appropriate signals into the nervous system to program the muscles to respond to fulfil your belief. The difference between an 8 iron and a 7 iron technically shows that if you put the two clubs in a swing machine the results would be different - the 7 iron would send the ball further.

The mind and body does not work like a machine. The inner mind will apply the right amount of energy to produce the shot you have selected. The club really makes little difference within common sense differences. The key to learn here is it is your belief, your confidence that determines the outcome.

Keep a Positive Mental Attitude

- Create a positive attitude
- Play your round against par. Concentrate on beating the course and not your opponent!

- Hit each shot as good as you can with a "so what" attitude, no matter what score you shoot relate to par as well as you can and learn from it.

- Play smart. Whether you are playing a hole, a round or a tournament, look for the positive to offset any negative.

- Picture a clear shot in your mind and see the exact shot you want to hit, giving yourself credit for thinking properly.

- Create an inner trance-like state. One way to trigger this state is to create an anchor by making an association with some action that will trigger this state of mind automatically before you tee off. I know people who have created this trigger by repeatedly tossing a ball in the air and then catching it. This act helps to focus you attention inwards away from any distractions in your environment.

- Remember to stay in a physical state of 'ready to go' ready to spring into action.

- Develop perseverance, gratitude, appreciation, respect and serenity.

Putting

Putting makes up about forty percent of the total shots you will play in a round of golf. It is therefore much more important than the length of your tee shot. It is a good idea to cultivate an effective practice routine and to give this area of the game a lot of attention. Your objective is to learn how to play with a narrow relaxed focus of mind; an empty mind, a positive belief and total confidence that you can 'Putt To Make It' or that 'Every Putt is a Green Light Putt'.

The single most important aspect you can develop which will transform your putting ability into one of putting excellence is to become confident on the putting green. Becoming a confident putter creates the belief that 'You Are a Great Putter'. Work through the following steps to enable this to happen for you. Do not move onto the next step until you have total mastery over the first step. CD4 is also used to create Perfect Putting.

You can achieve the state of mind of a perfect putter!

Practice Drill to become a Perfect Putter

1.   Practice from the shortest distance you can - say one foot or even nine inches from the hole until you can sink the putt every time.

2.   See the putt in your mind and let it go, putting to make it.

3.   Once you have achieved this, practice from a distance of between one to two feet away from the hole; do this until you achieve putting with ease from this distance.

4.   When you can do this try the same distance again with your eyes closed. Just look at the ball and then the target, close your eyes, focus on the target, see the putt and let it go. You will surprise yourself as you sink the putt.

5.   Repeat this drill up to about four feet away from the hole.

6.   To maintain confidence and positive belief in your putting maintain a practice from a distance of one to four feet away from the hole.

What you are doing is to prove to yourself that 'YOU CAN PUTT'.

You are developing a new confidence within you together with a belief that 'YOU ARE A GREAT PUTTER!' It is your state of mind that is the key to great putting.

Short range success builds confidence. It is confidence which creates a positive belief that you are a great putter. This new mental ability will enable you to play in tournaments as if you are on the practice green.

Remember in earlier chapters we learnt how the mind works. You will see that developing successful short range putting ability creates the message that will be sent to your unconscious mind 'putt the ball in the hole'. This is also why focusing on the target is so important in putting. You are telling you inner mind where to putt the ball.

Practice the ability to read the green for long putts

Instead of making lots of long putts towards the hole, change this to making long putts to reach the fringe of the other side of the green. Why do this? The reason is so that you develop the ability to make distance without the failure of not sinking the putt. Your new belief that you can sink the putt will still be in place. Everything is fine; you will still select your target and that is where the ball is going to go. This is a great drill for positive long putting and developing reading the green.

Practice Drill to Develop Trust and Inner Vision

1. Roll the ball towards the hole/target

2. Roll the ball again towards the hole with your eyes closed

This drill will teach you how to focus your mind on the target. You will send signals to your subconscious mind what you wish your body to perform for you. The hypothalamus in the brain will orchestrate an infinity of events to bring about the message you are holding in your conscious mind, within your frontal lobe, to bring about the outcome you require.

New pre-shot routine

Think only of the Target Routine. Play 18 holes using this new approach of only looking at the target.

The Traditional Pre Shot Method

1. Look at the Ball
2. Look at the Target
3. Look at the ball
4. Swing the putter and hit the ball

New Pre Shot Approach

1. Look at the ball
2. Look at the Target
3. Swing the putter and hit the ball

Select the smallest target you can focus upon

The other fact to consider is to select the smallest target that you can. You could select a blade of grass, a certain mark on the hole, a spike mark near the hole in line with your target. When you focus specifically on the smallest target the mind performs to its optimum.

Gain control by giving up control
Getting yourself out of the way

Will power has to be surrendered. Trying too hard is a recipe for disaster allowing the opportunity for many angry or self punishing emotions to be released. You will introduce doubt causing the tightening of the muscles. This causes tension and tension creates a negative cycle within the body. I am sure you all know that this negative cycle produces the ineffective golf swing, resulting in a poor unhappy game with higher scores than you would wish to have.

Your first instincts are the best

You are going to learn to trust your natural intuition. When you are approaching any shot your past memory has already established the best way for you take your next shot.

Respond to your mistakes with Acceptance

Key: respond with acceptance, stay in the present moment of no past no future only now. You need to learn to forget your last shot – good or bad.

Staying in the Present Moment

Your mind needs to learn to let go of the past. This includes whatever score you have just shot or whether your shot was a bad one or an excellent one. You need to say focused on this very shot. The future outcome is to be ignored, which includes "How am I doing with my score?" "How is my partner or opponent doing with their game?"

One Shot at a Time

The only reality you have is in the now. This very shot – see the target and hit the ball. That is all there is. Many books refer to the statement 'One shot at a Time'. Everything you have learnt relates to this statement which is referring to being in the now, not being concerned with the outcome or the goal, entering the zone to totally focus on where you are now.

Putting Routine

Physical Activity

1. Taking the grip
2. Taking the stance
3. Taking the practice swings

Mental Activity

1. Reading the green
2. Deciding on the line
3. Clearing the Mind
4. Putting to make it
5. Accepting the result

Putting should be your first step to becoming a great golfer. Once you have mastered putting move out from the hole in terms of distance to chipping onto the green. Once you have mastered chipping onto the green, master your irons starting from your nine iron until you arrive at your three iron. Finally finish with your drivers.

What you are doing is starting from mastering a nine inch putt. Yes you can sink the ball, you can do it!

Your next step is to move slowly further away from the putting green in terms of distance. The closer you are to the hole the less chance that a major error will occur. This will boost your self belief and confidence that you are a great golfer. Remember you are training your mind that you can do it, that you are a great golfer. When you do this your self belief will become rock solid.

You can do it and you will be programming yourself with this message of success. You will have a history of successful nine inch putts to prove it. Your mind is now in a positive state containing the belief you can do it.

The rest of your game will now naturally develop as you take more lessons with your Pro to build upon your technique. Technique on its own will not achieve the result you wish for, however technique plus a positive belief in your game of golf will create your very own Mastering the Inner Game of Golf. Have fun and smile.

Competitions with the Pros

In this chapter I have included two major golf championship competitions that many golfers have an interest in following; The Open Championship held in Scotland and The Women's British Open. What I am presenting is based purely upon speculation and is in not as a result of any personal interviews with the players I have made a reference to; I have guessed what was happening in the mind of the players. I have been able to maintain a neutral position as I have no preference towards any one particular player, having equal respect to all these superb players. The observations that I have made show the way the players appear to be playing in relation to their attitude and responses to outcomes, plus their responses to interviews held after or during the event.

This chapter has been included to illustrate many of the mind training skills I am presenting in this course. I have met a lot of players who enjoy their golf until it comes to competitions, when they engage in another emotional mode completely. This is when the golfer can get very serious creating a change to occur within their mind. This change in mental attitude causes many golfers to have serious problems with their thoughts and emotions. When a 'competition' looms on the horizon they can experience reactions such as sleepless nights, anxiety attacks and very tense golf rounds in their preparation for the event. What I am sharing with you in this chapter is that when 'competition' comes into the mind, the golfer can go to pieces. The only difference that has happened is they are now embracing a difference idea. As a result they put themselves at a disadvantage just through adopting a different attitude towards their golf game.

The main point to learn about playing in competitions is to develop the ability to treat the 'competition' exactly the same as if playing for fun. You will see that when the Pros have discovered that they have gone beyond any contention of winning their play changes to include enjoyment and fun, they start playing with a 'So What' attitude. It is through letting go of the mind's need to win and to achieve a result that they start performing at their best; they have re-entered the zone albeit by accident.

When this happens they experience the joy of golf with lower scores resulting as an insignificant consequence. There are many examples of this with the Pro players in the two championships you are about to read. Please enjoy this section whilst paying attention to what the golfers are saying and doing in relation to their results. I think this will illustrate the teaching points that are advisable to learn to become the best golfer you can become.

The 2009 Open Championship
Turnberry, Ayrshire, Scotland

The main focus of events in relation to this competition is about what is happening in the fourth round; the last day of the competition.

I will introduce you to a colourful player I expect you all know well and that is Rory Mcilroy from Northern Ireland. Rory went into the fourth round seven over par believing that he was out of contention for the competition. After he completed the round he was reported to be 'having a good laugh on the course', everyone could see he was thoroughly enjoying himself. As a result of letting go of the idea of winning, as there was nothing to try and achieve he was playing without a care. The result reflected this new attitude when he shot one over par in his last round, shooting seventy-one.

What would have been his result if he could have trained his mind to have the same attitude throughout the competition that he had when he started his fourth round? I don't know what attitude he had but the circumstances show us that he believed he was beyond winning the championship which enabled him to take 'one shot at a time' in a relaxed, happy, enjoyable manner. With the attitude he had in the fourth round the result was a by-product which was one shot over par.

Luke Donald from England on the third day approached his tee shot on the 12th and had something distract him or had a doubt or change of mind about what shot to play. He steps away from the tee, turns around, walks a few yards and turns back round to face the fairway. He then proceeds to make a few practice swings and re-approaches the tee to make a tremendous shot.

What can we learn from what Luke had done as this is the sign of a future champion? First of all when distracted he turned around, walked a few yards, turned back again and made several practice swings before he walked back up to tee to take his shot. This physical action will release any information that has entered his nervous system trapped in the muscles of his body before he re-programs his inner mind with the shot he now wants to make. The key tip here is 'any doubt or distraction that enters your mind just before the swing walk away and take some physical action to release and clear the mind and body before you take the shot'.

In the final round of the open Ross Fisher from England at the second hole was leading the day with 5 under, two shots in front of Tom Watson. He was playing amazing golf however he finished the day in eleventh place two over. No one will ever know what went wrong for him as he went on to drop seven shots.

We know that he was carrying a major distraction in his mind, his wife was about to give birth to a baby. How would you carry two major events in your life; leading the Open on the last day and being about to become a father? The press were having a field day with him and the night before he had his mind full with front page news about the dilemma. How would you be able to let this go, always waiting to hear the fantastic news at any time especially as he wanted to be at the birth? The other possibility is that he knew what his score was, allowing that to influence his game.

To suddenly know you could win the Open can dramatically change the mental game. Remembering the facts discovered through neuroscience that when the mind focuses on the goal the unconscious takes this information as a fact which causes the sports mode of excellence to switch off. This fact has been applied by the Japanese Olympic swimming team in their training preparation. This idea that the goal is near causes the information being sent to the motor cortex to change. The result is a sports performance mode of under achievement and unfocused play.

Another possibility is that knowing he was doing well his conscious mind's will could have come into play, allowing the personality to dominate and inflate his own ability. When the attitude of "I am invincible" happens you can enter a state of over focussing with the will trying to force the outcome. The personality can get carried away with the tremendous results of the last two holes going into a state of rapture, thinking it is invincible. When this euphoric state takes over, the individual takes unnecessary risks by holding a distorted belief in their ability causing what I call 'over positive play'.

What is really happening here is that you are allowing the idea of winning to become a message to your unconscious that you can relax 'don't bother with golf because it is over as 'I have won'. The inner mind will obediently obey you changing your state of being into non performance mode. The inner mind will then focus upon any other secondary idea you have previously presented it. In the case of Ross Fisher it would be becoming a father, not playing professional golf.

The only response to every experience you have when you are playing in a competition is to re-enter the zone. Your greatest ally is the inner zone. It will take over, lifting you to a state of excellence in performance, emotionally centred in a state of quite graceful contentment. Today commentators are catching onto this state and calling it serenity. You need to let go of your will, of your ego, allowing the zone to orchestrate the enormous amount of information required to bring about the desired goal, for your shot to hit your selected target. Get the will out of the way, staying in the present moment, with the mind state of 'only this shot now exists'. Learn to trust in the inner zone - only then can you let go.

The commentators were talking amongst themselves after a great tee shot on the sixth when Tom Watson produced a birdie opportunity after making the green with a lucky bounce just past the two bunkers that were just in front of the green. They said there will be a few guys praying for that sort of bounce. A Pro golfer recently said "The difference between praying in a church and praying on a golf course is that on the golf course you really mean it." The other commentators all laughed with one chipping in with "But they don't get answered".

This is the reality of most people's understanding of how the mind works. Hope and pray without belief. When you have proved to yourself that what you think about in a focused way creates your own reality, then you will have belief and faith that anything is possible. You will know that your thoughts are more than just thoughts. You will know that your thoughts land upon the inner realm of existence, which is boundless and orchestrates an infinity of events to manifest the material experience matching your original thoughts; this inner mind fulfils your original request or desire that was converted into thoughts. How amazing you are. This truth is now scientifically explained in quantum physics.

Be careful not to pollute your orders to the inner zone because it will not edit them. It will accept your thoughts without question unless they meet deeply rooted self sabotaging beliefs you hold about yourself. See rule 4 in How The Mind Works. Opposing ideas cannot be held at the same time. This is why you need to practice the exercises in the back of this book, especially 'Creating a Positive Self Image' where you create new movies in your mind with new positive behaviours for the life you wish to create. The outcomes you choose now to experience in these new movies you make in your mind are taken into the inner zone every time you use one of the five CDs that accompany this course. It is also worth looking at rule No. 5 'Once an idea has been accepted by the subconscious it remains until it is replaced by another idea' and rule No. 7 'Each suggestion acted upon creates less opposition to successive suggestions'.

Becoming an excellent golfer also has to do with becoming an excellent person. Develop strong belief in the inner power of your mind through proof. Become the scientist carrying out experiments to prove the workings of the mind. I have provided you with all the tools you need to do this, it is up to you to use them. One last point here; don't try and run before you can walk, please take small steps at first. This approach will provide you with all the proof you need and once you have proof you can then develop strong belief and trust in how your mind works in relation to the whole of existence. This will create a calm, relaxed, happy, positive, trusting golfer.

England's Chris Wood had a tremendous round shooting 67 in the fourth round of the Open producing one eagle, four birdies, ten pars and three bogeys. His final position in the 2008 Open was fifth. Having achieved third position in the 2009 leaving him just one shot behind the winner in this very difficult competition, this tremendous result where Chris shot three under on the day must make him a future champion, being that he is only 21 years old. His game was positive, consistent and he appeared to be applying 'one shot at a time'. He had a tremendous caddy with him who would not let him look at the leader board at the point he was tied leader at the 13th.

Let's look at how Chris could have made that extra shot. Having just birdied the 17th he was two under with the goal in sight. The 18th is a 461 yard par four. Chris must know that he is playing extremely well. Chris drives off producing a safe shot that runs just off the fairway into the semi-rough. He produced a beautiful second shot, a wonderful strike out of the rough, with a very strong wind behind the ball, causing it to hit the 18th green running off the back downhill into the fringe. This left him an approximate fifteen yard uphill chip into the wind. This was his second shot on a par four. I think most good players would be happy with this situation - only a chip and a putt to make par. As Chris was walking towards the 18th green to take his third shot he was greeted by tremendous applause and appreciation from a crowd that treated him like a famous celebrity. The chip he was about to make carried great importance as it could have been good enough for him to win the Open. He had to chip over a steep slope to land on the edge of the green which was sloping downhill to the pin. Carefully assessing his shot he swings the club and falls far short leaving a three metre putt. Putting for par Chris missed it by a whisker; leaving a simple tap in. This resulted in Chris dropping a shot, making a bogey.

The interesting thing is that Chris only had three bogeys in the whole round, one being on the final hole, the 18th. Did Chris get over excited when he was teeing off from the 18th, realising this after the second shot onto the green where the ball had gone too far. As a result then over compensated through holding back a bit on his shot to steady himself? Through under chipping the shot onto the green and failing to make the putt caused him to drop a shot. This is one possibility.

When interviewed he said "I played so good all day, really steady, I never felt like making any mistakes. I felt really comfortable out there". He was also comparing how he got pipped to the post by Ian Poulter last year and that it was this situation that was going through his mind at the time. He also did say that the experience he had last year helped prepare him for this year.

When Chris was being interviewed after completing the fourth round he was lying fifth with one under. At that time there were three players tying first position with three under. Tom Watson, the last player out and favourite for the day was at the 12th. Lee Westwood was at the 13th with three under and Stewart Cink was lying fourth with two under at the 15th. Speculating on where he would end up he said "There are a few tough holes out there which those players have to experience so I could be one or two short, but you never know."

The truth of the final results was that he was one shot down; he was right in his perception. The main point to consider for us is revealed in Chris's remark about how he could not get out of his mind the last year's situation where he got pipped to the post by Ian

Poulter. This instruction was accepted by the inner zone through his unconscious mind and produced exactly the same result for him this year. The lesson here is confirmation in the chapter on how the mind works in rule number two, 'What is expected tends to be realised'. The things that I have feared have come upon me! Was this not the fear that Chris held as he approached the eighteenth? He told us indirectly it was.

The Last Two Holes

The 2009 Open was a championship to remember for many reasons. Two young up and coming champions England's Chris Wood and Italy's amateur Matteo Manassero, who finished plus two winning the leading amateur silver medal award, both shone like stars.

It is on the last two holes where we are going to focus our attention, for this is where the mental game really comes into play and can make the difference between winning or not. The key players are all within two shots of each other, the crowd are excited as the intensity builds. The atmosphere is electric. What you will need to do to is to be able to play under these atmospheric conditions staying within the zone and enjoying your play. This is where your visualisation exercise of making the movie in your mind and then taking it into the zone using the CD set is used. You are going to rehearse the outcome to prepare yourself for the experience when it occurs for you.

Tom Watson had just putted a par on the 15th to drive off from the 16th tied in lead position with Lee Westwood at two under. Stuart Cink playing consistently had not drawn much attention from the commentators and was quietly drawing close to the leaders as he was at the 18th just one shot behind the leaders at one under par. Stuart played a tremendous birdie with extreme calm and confidence on the 18th to finish up in joint lead position at two under with Tom Watson who had two holes still to play.

Lee Westwood had an eagle putt opportunity on the 17th that ended up on the lip of the cup. He now tied in first place at two under with Tom Watson and Stuart Cink. However Lee knew the importance of the eagle putt and was devastated at not making it. We will not know what thoughts went through his head at that moment but he was displaying his bitter disappointment for everyone to see as he walked away from the green. Lee put his right hand up to his forehead in a gesture of disbelief about what had just happened. Will he allow this to influence his final hole?

Lee teed off with a great drive; his ball hit the middle of the fairway disappointingly to be drawn into a bunker. His second shot was brave and spectacular; using an eight iron he just passed the six foot high lip of the bunker to land on the green. His first putt was about twenty yards and finished up five foot past the hole. He missed his par opportunity to leave him to finish on a bogey and one under for the competition; the same position as Chris Woods.

Lee has a tremendous consistent game with a calm unshakable manner. Although he was disappointed at not winning he is always optimistic looking forward to the next tournament. Both Lee

Westwood and Chris woods are great examples of how to retain an attitude of 'one shot at a time'.

Tom Watson finished on the 17th leading with three under after making a birdie putt. Winning the Open depended on the eighteenth par four hole. Leaving his driver in his bag he teed off with a hybrid club to play safe. His shot landed on the middle of the fairway leaving a one hundred and seventy yard shot to the front of the green. The second shot hit the green only to roll off past the flag, down a gentle slope landing two inches into the slight rough past the fringe, just as Lee Westwood had previously done. He only has to chip the ball fifteen feet, make the putt to win the championship. Tom is renowned to be an excellent chipper of the ball. He left his wedge in the bag taking a putter to the ball hitting the ball past the flag to leave about a five foot putt to win. He missed the shot by about two inches to leave him with a four hole play off with Stuart Cink.

In the play off Stuart remained solid and consistent where Tom appeared to have lost his resolve playing into the rough several times. Stuart went on to win the Open by a large margin. Tom was so despondent his shots were very out of character, under distance and into troubled areas.

What is interesting is that on the eighteenth hole in the play off he had to chip over a bunker onto the green. Unfortunately he under played the chip shot. This left him another very long chip onto the green. At this stage Stuart was waiting to take his final birdie shot to win the tournament. Tom knowing it was all over made a casual chip without any thought, ending his game in style for he left his ball beside the cup for a final two foot putt.

The point to notice here is that when Tom had stopped trying to compete he played automatically from within his unconscious with the mind out of the way. Had he played like this on the eighteenth in the fourth round when he used a putter to play onto the green instead of chipping on he could have won the day.

Full credit goes to Stuart Cink as he kept his mind strong playing his normal consistent game to comfortably win. He was not fazed emotionally by the crowd who were in full support of Tom Watson to win. He also experienced the full support of the crowd the day before when he was partnered with Lee Westwood; he totally accepted this experience. Although he won the championship it was his ability to stay calm talking 'one shot at a time' that I believe was the factor for his success.

What can we learn from what the players say?

John Senden from Australia said after shooting 66 on the first day "I felt good about my game; the golf course was just beautiful". When he was asked what is the key to maintaining his momentum he replied "Look at what I did well today. Tomorrow is a brand new day so I will just go out and play my game and not worry about what everyone else is doing".

On the second day of the Open Ross Fisher shot 68 finishing with a birdie, birdie and par. He said he felt like he was playing on his own being able to stay focused and patient, playing 'one shot at a time'.

We can learn from these two players who were performing at their best as they all had similar remarks which were 'just having fun and playing in the present moment just one shot at a time'. In achieving ignoring the goal and the comparison of results they produced their best golf.

Lee Westwood at the end of the third day was playing two under when he was asked "What sort of numbers do you have in your mind, what score do you think is achievable in the final round?" He replies something like "I don't have a number at all in mind, that goes for links golf and any major championship. Just go out and do the same thing as normal which is to play 'one shot at a time' one hole at a time, just doing the best on that particular hole". On another occasion he said words similar to "Just be patient, not think I have to do too much".

The lesson we can learn from Lee is don't try and push or force your game as you will make mistakes. Regard competitions in the same way as when you go out and play for fun. The other key point is not to become attached to a particular expected score because if you don't make it you will become disappointed. This will lead to anxiety which will turn into a tension to create a bad swing which will result in even worse results.

Ross Fisher had this to say "I tried to stay chilled, relaxed and enjoy every moment".

Mathew Goggin says "Stay within yourself and be as calm as possible".

Tom Watson from the USA when he was leading the Open at the end of the third round was interviewed and asked "How will you cope with your nerves tomorrow?" he replied "I'm going to be in the present mind set. Today was probably the most serene I have ever been on the golf course. It was a delightful walk out there today. I'm going to try and keep the serenity going on the next 18 holes. I'm going to keep to my game plan which is working."

The Women's 2009 British Open Championship
Royal Lytham & St Annes

Christina Kim from the USA, regarded as the iron lady of the PGA MPA tour having played 95 matches from 2003 to 2005, approached a long putt on the 10th green. She played about one foot short and then talking to herself out loud, she said with a tone of annoyance "You'd think after ten holes I'd get it to the hole." What is interesting is that on the remaining eight holes she continuously kept putting short. Her inner mind really did obey her very strong will.

Self talk has to be examined very carefully. Do you talk to yourself in a reprimanding manner? Remember the unconscious mind takes all of your comments literally as commands to what you want to achieve. There is no discernment in the unconscious – it responds literally. If you beat yourself up your inner zone will respond by creating situations where you experience results that will fall short of your expectations. Your inner mind has dutifully obeyed you, yes you have within you the genie of the universe and you wonder why you are not getting what you want! Try giving it positive commands with outcomes that you wish to have. In reality you have to first discover that the inner realm exists and this is how the outcomes in your life are created. Once you have proof you can then develop trust in something greater than yourself. When you do this your golf will improve. However this is not the most important gain you will experience, no not just the score but your new found relaxation, emotionally centred with a focused mind where nothing in the environment bothers or disturbs you. You discover the joy of golf not for winning but for the sheer pleasure of playing. Winning when you experience this state of being becomes a by product.

On the tenth green in the third round Song-Hei Kim from Korea made a brilliant 20 foot plus birdie putt keeping her one under for the day. She has the joint highest recorded putt rate at 1.74 which means she gets down in less than two putts most of the time. This is a great lesson to be learnt about developing the short game, especially positive belief in putting, as this is often the least glamorous but often the deciding factor to winning or losing tournaments. The ladies winner Catriona Matthew won the championship with the magic wand on the putting green. Many western golf experts are noticing that in the recent years there is flood of eastern golfers from Korea etc. filling the top positions in the championships. I believe because of their culture they have a greater affinity with their relationship to the inner zone. It is this relationship that will make the difference.

On the 16th hole Italian Giulia Sergas had a double bogey having missed a three foot putt. Her body language was showing that the outcome of the last three holes, where she had dropped a few shots had attached itself to her emotionally. The outcome was that she was showing signs of being despondent and depressed. She was unable to let her bad spell go. I have no idea what thoughts she was having but there was no mistaking her playing attitude to that of a person who was defeated. The sign of a good player is the ability to refresh themselves and by the 18th she had done just that. Her body language had improved with a smile as she made a tremendous second shot onto the green five feet from the flag. She missed the birdie putt to finish with a par and three over for the day.

What happens in this situation and let's face it we have all experienced the few holes that do not go to plan; into the rough, into the bunker off the back of the green, the missed two foot putt. The only approach is to refresh your resolve, accept what has happened letting the past shot go, re-enter the zone and start from the now. You have to let go of the desired outcome to win. In Giulia's situation she started the third round as joint leader with three under and was now playing three over. Attachment to outcome will destroy you in this situation. I recently played with a fellow club golfer who after watching two players in match play at the fourteenth stated "It will be difficult for our club member to win the game as he was three holes down". I said "Anything was possible because the game was not yet over and there are four holes still left to play". He replied "Yes but I have been in that position many times and it is very difficult to come back when you are three holes under". I did not reply because his mind was fixed about what happens in this situation.

105

I hope you can see that if you hold a belief like this your inner mind will create that outcome for you. In the case of my fellow golfer he knew this was the case but was ignorant as to the reason why the outcome was almost like he believed it to be.

Christina Kim, a very animated player who talks to her ball all the time has worked very hard at her game this year feels that it is just starting to pay off. She finished in second position with one under for the day. Her approach to her game is to stay patient and take just 'one shot at a time'. When asked "How do you think you will play tomorrow?" she replied "That's a good seventeen hours from now and I refuse to think about that now. I'm just here to soak in the joy right now and hopefully go up and get a pie". I congratulate her on her ability to stay in the present moment. This is an example of how to remain focused in the now without attachment to the desire of winning.

Catriona Matthew played a fantastic calm round of golf to finish with four under in the lead position before going into the final round. She played sensibly with good straight hitting, good thinking and good putting. There was a calmness about her giving her the confidence to play in a controlled well thought out way. This produced consistent golf without the need to take any risks. When she was asked how she was feeling on the course her reply was "Not so calm as I may have looked, I tried to stay relaxed but it is difficult out there, however I just try and keep going." She said her game plan was to try and hit the fairways and keep out of the bunkers. "If you go in the bunkers here you are looking at bogeys or even double bogeys. Try and keep the bogeys off the card and have a par on every hole". Her view was that although she was three shots ahead as she entered the fourth round she had to be careful as the course is full of danger. She said this means you have to really concentrate on every hole. The truth of her fourth round reflected her concerns she had voiced at her interview as she had a continuous problem with hitting the fairways. Could this have been the conditioning she gave to her inner mind the night before her final round?

With the experience of many competitions she said that she had learnt to have the attitude to stay patient if you have a bad start and remember that everyone else is nervous as well as you. Just hang in there as you never know what is going to happen. Do not react to any bad or good play and do not get too far ahead of yourself, just wait and see what happens.

The final round was full of excitement as the excellent women golf contenders gave Catriona a run for her money. Although she lost her ability to stay on the fairway her putting was golden, like a magic wand, which defiantly clinched the day. She finished a clear winner with three under with Karrie Webb Australia's three times previous winner making par. Catriona joins an elite band of winners for this championship, surely a tremendous inspiration for lady golfers in the UK as the first Scot to win a major championship and the fourth Briton to do so.

When asked how she coped with her shaky start she replied "My husband *(who was her caddy)* reminded her to take one shot at a time". This had the effect of steadying her.

The quality she carried within her performance was a serenity just like the quality that Tom Watson had in the third round of the men's Open. This quality can only come from going beyond the golfing technique, the personal body fitness or the ego's personality as it is what it universally available to us all – the realm of 'the inner zone'. It is this aspect that will keep you calm after the bad shot, transport you through the obstacles and challenges you are bound to face in competition golf.

Developing attitudes that will keep you in the zone

The following attitudes, acceptance, gratitude, enjoyment and enthusiasm will help you when you are playing golf to stay connected to the inner zone.

Acceptance will help you remain in the present moment. Without acceptance it is very easy to slip into negativity based upon the past or the future, allowing the result of your last shot or circumstances outside of you within your environment to influence you negatively.

Remember influences like other people are by nature outside of your control. You do have influence and can affect others. The best way to do this is through being positive towards them even if they being hostile towards you. Accepting what is happening now will create a positive feedback loop towards everything that is, or has just happened, in a positive unconscious way. This approach enables you to let go and become focused again with a clear empty mind ready to program your next shot. Negative emotions such as anger or frustration will never arise when you learn to accept what is. Freedom from negative emotions enables a relaxed body, the perfect state of being for the golf swing.

Enjoyment of your golf naturally arises when you have acceptance as it allows you let go of judgement from your mind. This has the effect of freeing your mind to do what it is meant to do; formulate your next shot. When you let go of the ego, the mind becomes clear and the inner zone will be able to flow into you.

When you have this state of mind you will experience what Tom Watson experienced in day three of the 2009 Open in Scotland, a state he described as serenity. I hope you had the opportunity of watching this championship as you will remember how he glided round the course as if lifted by a greater energy than his own. He was really enjoying the golf, the crowd, the other players, the weather, in fact everything as he was out of himself allowing the flow to take over. This state of being is what you will experience when you can apply acceptance, allow your mind to become focused and free and enter the inner zone. In fact you are making a space inside of you for the inner zone to enter you.

How do you get the crowd on your side at a big competition? First of all you have to accept their reaction to whatever is happening, they might be cheering for the player next to you. Accept it and enjoy their support for him or her. When you do this you are removing your ego's need for approval and your own need of being liked. An interesting thing will happen; you are sending them appreciation and this quality will be returned to you through the inner zone. We are able to communicate with each other emotionally without touching each other. The power of the crowd's energy will affect the players. If the crowd is against or on your side accept it and enter the inner zone with appreciation for them.

The inner zone connects everything equally without prejudice therefore whatever thoughts you send others will return to you in some way or another. Over time the crowd will start to appreciate your respectful manner and start rooting for you. Then you can be grateful of their positive desire for your success. This is very real and will help you in competitions to embrace this attitude and collective social understanding of how others can lift your game. The truth is that when you are focused on the inside into the inner zone you no longer become dependent on the outside environment for your energy lift, having your ego boosted by others because if they don't support you and instead send you negativity you will be devastated. The inner zone will give you everything you ever need to play excellence in your game of golf. This will release you from mental and emotional anguish. You will have no concern for what is happening in the environment outside of you i.e. the people by the first tee, the crowd at the 18th green. We are all connected equally through the inner zone through the space of existence. Football clubs tend to do better at home than away because of the power of the positive desire of the crowd sending the players energy to succeed.

The other consideration for crowds or spectators on the golf course is to again appreciate them with respect because without their interest in the golfer and the golf tournament there would not be any competition as they make a contribution to enable you to play. Through being connected to the inner zone you will be in a higher state of consciousness than that of the mind's judgement energy created by the crowd, you will in fact be sending them a joyful experience when they watch you play.

Enthusiasm naturally arises from your passion of playing golf. When you practice acceptance you remain joyful in the present moment, relaxed and focused, always open to the new. The new will be your goals but they will no longer possess you and stress you to a state of being miserable, they will transform into a positive enthusiasm. It is this state that will enable you to continue evolving in your game taking the feedback from your game after the eighteen holes have been played and develop a training programme for yourself, to enable your continuous improvement.

Enthusiasm brings an enormous self empowerment into what you do. Achieving excellence becomes a natural phenomena, a by product of your ability to enter the zone, stay in the flow, maintain acceptance and experience the joy of golf. When you have discovered this art you will do less and less and achieve more and more because it will be the greater energy you have connected with that is now expanding your life.

A Final Thought

I have enjoyed writing this course immensely as it contains everything I have ever learnt since I qualified as a hypnotherapist practicing at a Harley Street clinic in 1986. What you are presented with in this book are short cuts that really work based upon the success of others. The people I have helped are helping you now as they have proven that the methods and techniques are effective in bringing change to your life.

Will this course work for you? This is only decided by one fact and one fact alone, which is dependent upon your ability of surrendering that what you think you already know, the limitations held within your ego.

Please enter into what is presented to you with an open mind. Yes it will then pleasantly surprise you; it will start working in a very subtle way, automatically appearing in your game of golf.

There is one other important ingredient you have to do to achieve mastery over your mind and that is simple. You have to take action. The action you need to take is to actually do it! Many people just read the book making judgements of agreement or disagreement as they do so without trying out the exercises. The problem with this is that your ego is just looking for confirmation that you know it all; there is nothing else for you to learn. This approach will achieve nothing and you will indeed prove the course does not work.

I encourage you to have an open mind. Try everything out for yourself, keep what works and most importantly enjoy yourself in the process. I wish you every success from the bottom of my heart.

Self Help Exercises

Breathing Meditation

Breathing exercise to induce the Alpha state

Deep breathing from the diaphragm is the key to relaxation on the golf course. A full deep breath increases the amount of oxygen as the body begins to function effectively, especially during mental activity.

To feel the full effect of correct breathing, place your hand over your navel and imagine you have a balloon in your stomach. Breathe deeply through the nose - as the balloon inflates your hand moves outwards. As you breathe out imagine the balloon deflating and feel the abdomen falling.

Before starting any exercise on relaxation always take three full deep breaths - and feel the tension and negative energy drain away on the out breath, breathing in positive energy on the in breath. Once you have learnt this simple breathing method to achieve meditation try using it with your CD1 - getting your mind to work for you.

Here is the simple procedure

1. Imagine the balloon in your abdomen as this is where you transfer your consciousness. Breathe in relaxation and positive energy and hold the breath for three seconds.

2. Breathe out, letting go of any tension and negative energy - feel the balloon deflate - and again hold the breath for three seconds. Become aware of the precise moment of stillness.

3. Breathe in again - be aware of the air filling your lungs - hold for three seconds.

4. Breathe out with a sigh - feel the air leaving your body. Hold for three seconds.

5. Breathe in - be aware of the air flowing in. Hold for three seconds.

6. Breathe out with a sigh and feel the tension draining away.

Using Visualisation in conjunction with CDs 2 to 5

You will create a visualisation at home, a movie in your mind of what you want to happen in your game. This method is also ideal to be used whenever you have just had a technical coaching lesson from your PGA professional. Create a new visualisation playing golf in a new way to include what the lesson has just taught you.

This brain training exercise has the effect of creating a new neural pathway in your brain. When this new memory has been created it will act as an instruction program to produce the bodily outcome in your golf swing automatically when you are on the golf course.

CD2 is used for new outcomes you want in your Long Game

CD3 is used for new outcomes you want in your Short Game

CD 4 is used for new outcomes you want in your Putting

CD 5 is used for outcomes to Tournaments and Competitions

The following exercise 'Creating a Positive Self-Image' illustrates how to use this method in detail. You can use this exercise for anything you want to change in your game of golf or in fact in your life. All you have to do is focus on one aspect at a time for example if you have trouble with anger after a bad shot use the exercise to see yourself responding in a new calm way, accepting what has just happened.

The key to your success is to only work on one thing at a time.

Creating a Positive Self-Image

When you are experiencing negative feelings about yourself the following exercise will help you regain a positive self image. This will have a knock on effect of re-establishing your positive sense of self worth. This exercise is very good if you wish to create a new behaviour or experience new positive emotions on the golf course or when you are entering competitions and tournaments. This exercise will transform negative conditioning and negative self beliefs. It is especially helpful in transforming your nerves into a positive signal when you are playing in competitions.

When you feel good about yourself your life condition will increase and your awareness will expand. What is happening? You are once again opening your heart to allow the inner zone resource to transform your negative emotions into positive emotions, especially self appreciation and self love. When you are really stuck and are unable to start this exercise because you feel so negative, use your breathing exercise to help relax you or use CD1 to lift you. This will expand your consciousness, increasing your awareness.

1.   Imagine yourself as you would ideally like to be. Think about how you would look if you were as happy and confident as you wanted to be. How would you walk? What would you wear? What expressions are on your face? Where do you go? How do you play your Golf? How do you swing the club? Take as much time as you need to see how you look when you are confident and full of self-esteem.

116

2. When you know what you will look like, make a little movie clip of yourself in your imagination, happy, confident, focused and self-assured.

3. You are now going into the zone by either using the breathing meditation or our CD1 or any of the five CDs.

4. When you are in the zone imagine stepping into yourself in that movie. See what you see, hear what you hear and feel the confidence of being there and enjoying being exactly how you want to be.

5. Imagine waking up tomorrow as your ideal self feeling this good, and imagine the day going exactly as you want it to when you play your next round of golf.

In order to get a maximum benefit from this technique, please use it daily for at least a week. Keep on using it for a minimum period of 21 days to form a new neural pathway in your brain, or more often if you want to. What you are doing in step 1 and 2 is creating a new behaviour in your conscious mind you wish to have in your life. In the steps 3 to 5 you are then sending this information in the form of a movie to your inner unconscious mind. As the unconscious mind responds beautifully to pictures it will understand this as a direct instruction as to what you wish it to produce for you in your behaviour, the action you take through your body.

You can take your positive movie with you when you play golf and run it in your mind whenever you need to strengthen your self image or dissolve negative emotions.

It is this method of creative visualisation you will use to create new golfing outcomes in your game. Use this method to create the result you want in your golf game in conjunction with CDs 2 to 5.

Changing Negative Internal Dialogue

Whenever you find yourself using your inner voice to talk about your situation in a negative way, listen to the voice that you can hear, remembering what it sounds like and then create a new voice to talk to yourself. The difference is that this new voice will be positive and will talk to you in ways to make you feel better about yourself; it will be on your side.

You can still hear exactly the same words and learn from whatever you are thinking but there is no need to feel bad unnecessarily! You are going to be creative and using the new voice you are going to say positive things to yourself to make you feel good about yourself. A good way to find a better form of words is to ask yourself how you would talk to a younger person whom you were helping to deal with a problem. Therefore instead of cursing or nagging yourself, try using kinder and more encouraging words to guide you towards what you want.

The Exercise to Change Negative Self Talk

- I want you now to think of the last time that you used your inner voice to talk to yourself or others. Remember what you were saying to yourself; remember the specific sentence you used, or type of statement you would have said to yourself.

- Repeat the statement that you made to yourself but change the tone of voice. Keep repeating exactly the same words, but make the tone of the voice different. Make it excited or happy. Make it funny or friendly. Make it sound like a cartoon character. Experiment by using all sorts of different tones of voice with exactly the same words until you find a tone that makes you feel completely different and one that brings you positive feelings.

- Now choose another voice. Choose an encouraging voice, the voice of a friend or a film star, or a voice with an accent you really like. You can play your inner voice in many more ways. You can speed it up or slow it down. You can make it higher or lower.

- Keep changing it until you find the characteristics that make it friendly, supportive and most of all loving and kind.

119

About the Author

Robert Bourne is an author, resource manager for organisations, a spiritual course creator, healer and Reiki Master Teacher. He began his career in sports psychology, hypnosis, psychotherapy and NLP gaining an honours degree for his thesis on Auto-suggestion in 1986.

After studying family systems, human communications and the Process of Change with Virginia Satir, the world's leading family therapist, he was appointed consultant psychotherapist and hypnotherapist at Harley Street's renowned Bluestone Clinic where conventional and alternative medical practitioners work together.

Robert went on to teach Ericksonian Hypnosis and NLP (Neural Linguistic programming for the Creation of Excellence) at Regents Park College. In 1995 an inner change in consciousness was experienced revealing Robert's true mission as a spiritual teacher and guide to other seekers.

Robert, author and course creator for Naturally You Publishing, is currently living in Devon in the UK. Robert's life's purpose is to offer teachings and energy experiences to bring about a change in higher consciousness for the individual. The vision is to enable you to create Personal Excellence through awakening an inner higher state of consciousness within you.

The Evolution of 'Into The Zone'
Mastering the Inner Game of Golf

In the last few years Robert has enjoyed learning the game of golf. He very quickly realised that this sport was very dependent upon three things; your technical ability, your physical state with its core stability and most importantly your state of mind.

Robert applied his ability to access inner states of consciousness which resulted in happy playing and lower scores although still playing with a high handicap. Fellow golfers would also benefit often saying things like "Thank you, since playing with you the other week my game is back on track as you have somehow sorted my head out". Robert decided to share this gift with as many sports people as he could, hence the creation of the revolutionary interactive courses 'INTO THE ZONE'. The first interactive course created especially for sports is called 'Mastering The Inner Game of Golf'.

Robert would like to share the following with you

"The creation of value is always the first consideration when creating interactive courses. It makes no difference if you wish to learn how to heal or become the best you can be in your chosen sport, the goal is always the same; and that goal is to enter into a higher consciousness than you are currently living your life by. When you do this new solutions automatically appear without the use of will power."

About the Author

"I am devoted to sharing this blissful inner connection of purity with you. I think that most people are settling for a life far less than they deserve, whether this is in their relationships, in their career, in their social, family or sporting life, or even within their finances.

Settling for only a part of your dreams will never make you happy. Settling for unhappy relationships only serves to limit your potential as the 'Unique Individual' that you are; you then tend to under achieve within your work, finances, sports, social and all creative aspects of your life.

Getting yourself to take action enables you to make anything happen that you really wish for; this reality I am sure you can already understand. The key to taking the best action for you comes in first removing any emotional limitations that you may have through connecting you with a greater inner consciousness than your own ego.

The secret to your happy existence therefore lays in the inner quality of your emotional experiences and in having the wisdom to make the right choices in each moment of your existence.

Then your life will then take on a new meaning, moving beyond your personal and social conditioning into unshakable happiness and personal enlightenment.

When you have discovered this beautiful inner realm your limitations and illusions will completely disappear!"

I wish you every success from the bottom of my heart
My deepest respect - Robert Bourne

Lightning Source UK Ltd.
Milton Keynes UK
20 December 2010

164658UK00010B/176/P